Writin

As a scribe of Higher Dimensional understanding, Beverly Thompson has done an outstanding job of not only bringing forth questions, but also of inscribing answers to aid in our Homeward journey. Above and beyond what heretofore we have called Truth, lies a whole *new* frontier of consciousness. And with our rising awareness of the new frontier come many questions and far too few answers.

Beverly Thompson is, in my opinion, an empowered pioneer of the new "guidebooks" into the fifth dimension of consciousness and beyond. The whole world is rapidly changing and so is each and every individual. We (humanity) are waking up to the vast love of the Universal Source, and each of us are yearning to know "how" to become one with that Love!

Beverly Thompson has inscribed a valuable guidebook to help us achieve the next step. I commend her for her clarity, humility and courage in bringing forth this very inspiring book.

— Rev. Marian Y. Starnes, founder of The Brigade of Light and author of *Letters from Summerland*

10.14.07
Paula - The greatness of your life lies in the wonderment of your joy expressed in and through you. Be present / you are a present through your presence.
Life is Incredible
Enjoy !!!
Beverly Thompson

Writings of the
Mystery
of the
Universes
A Prophecy Fulfilled

Writings of the
Mystery of the Universes
A Prophecy Fulfilled

by

Beverly J. Thompson

The Gathering Press

Writings of the
MYSTERY
of the
UNIVERSES

A Prophecy Fulfilled

by Beverly J. Thompson

Copyright © 2007 Beverly Thompson

ISBN 978-0-9794928-3-9

Published Spring 2007

Published by
The Gathering Press
Greenville, SC
www.thegatheringofangels.com

Contents of this book are copyrighted. No part may be reproduced by mechanical means, photocopy or computer without written authorization of the publisher (except for brief quotations by reviewers).

To order more copies of this book, please visit the author's web site:

www.thegatheringofangels.com.

Edited and designed by Tony Stubbs, *www.tjpublish.com*

Cover artwork by Beverly J. Thompson and Sharon Free, Sharon Free Designs, *www.thecreativediva.com*

Printed in the United States of America and United Kingdom

Contents

Foreword xii
Preface xiv
About the Author xvi
A Prophecy Fulfilled xviii
1 - Book of Kings 1
    Prophecy of the birth of The New Age
2 - The Grand Force 5
    Powers that are bestowed upon all people of this planet Earth
3 - Book of the Records 8
    Humanity in the making
4   Book of the Ages I 12
    The work of the Soltecs who established the teachings of the Essenes
5   Book of the Ages II 14
    Basic element of light
6   Book of the Song 17
    Continued teachings and truth of the Essenes
7   Book of Alignment 19
    Continued teachings of the Essenes, the processes of integration
8   Book of Genesis 22
    Open manifestation
9   Book of Winter 25
    The plan for manna, energized form
10 Book of Memory 28
    The Brotherhood of Creative Forces in the development of the new species of man
11 Book of Wonders 31
    Philosophies of the ancients in the making of the biological form of man
12 Book of Tomorrow 34
    Expansion of Creator in the physical
13 Book of Eternal Life 36
    All existence is the thoughts of Creator

14 Book of Myopia 39
    Life is everything
15 Book of Eternal Life from the Pharaohs of Avalon .. 41
    Life is an open-ended existence
16 Book of Divine Surrender 43
    An ancient book used in making the Declaration of Independence (of the USA)
17 Book of Divine Resurrection 46
    Soul expression and communication
18 The Apex of Adam 48
    "The Story of the Bucket" by Eurocles
19 Book of the Holy Grail 51
    An invitation by Anami to set up a communication network on the sharing of life
20 Know Thyself 53
21 Book of Titles 55
    Mankind is a combination of their many tasks
22 Book of the Azores 57
    A call for a new Earth and a new spirit of being, for mankind to cease from its destruction
23 Book of Tibet 60
    The biology of what is called "Plan 2"
24 The Forces of Evil 63
    Earth changes because of planet dwellers and their technologies
25 Book of Entrapment 68
    A call for the return of the light
26 Book of the Covenant 73
    The archangels make a covenant
27 Book of the Road to Beth-le-hem 75
    Story about a people who once lived in Northern Africa
28 Book of the Turban 78
    A once thriving ancient community
29 Book of the Dream 82
    The story of Antibus and his technology of spirit

30 Book of the Renaissance 84
    The divine rights by "The Knights of Splendor"
31 Book of Innocence 88
    The Monrovian Beings
32 Story of Heaven Eleven 91
    A story about a ship before the Ice Age
33 The Ides of March 94
    Europeans who were to be true to themselves and their beliefs
34 Book of Geldeiah 96
    Star men came to rescue man but found that man is a powerful light force
35 Book of Orion 100
    Beings from Orion came to this planet to start a new race and were called the Gods of Abraham
36 The Book of Isaiah 103
    The process of reproduction
37 Book of the Rainbow 107
    The birth of the plant kingdom
38 Book of the Journey 111
    The Rasputens, the form givers
39 Book of Genes 115
    A discussion of the magnetic clock with the body structure
40 Book of Illumined Truth 118
    Basic light as a rainbow of colors and frequencies
41 Book of Blue 120
    "Clear as blue"
42 Book of Letters 123
    Communication through symbols
43 Book of Gibraltar 126
    Anatomy of mankind
44 Book of Anatomy 130
    Liquid crystals hold patterns of creation
45 Book of Zep Tepi 133
    The new beginning

46 Book of Jerusalem 136
    The true nature of what is Jerusalem
47 The Night of the Dream 139
    Soul consciousness
48 Story of the Night Catcher 141
    The interconnectedness of the Divine Plan through a soul's choices
49 Book of Jonas 143
    The idea of symbolism by Jonas
50 Book of the Nightingale 146
    Inner earth beings and their story
51 Book of the Assembly 150
    The Tall Ones from inner earth, their life and job
52 Book of the Emerald Jewel 153
    This most magnificent Earth
53 Book of Stars 156
    Written by Aristotle on basic physics of sound and light travel
54 Book of Nature 158
    Recordings by Artemis – electromagnetic pulses and earth's energy
55 Book of Time 160
    Time: what it is and how it is used
56 Book of the Angelic Kingdom 164
    Why archangels exist
57 - Book of Celebration 167
    The Oconee Native Americans give their thanks
58 Book of the Oceans 169
    Waters of the Earth
59 The Night of Surrender 172
    Man shall treat this Mother Earth with respect
60 Book of Gibraltar, Part 2 175
    Our sun

61 Book of the Angelic Forces 178
    Angels exist to assist all of creation
62 The Book of Champions 180
    The story of a young boy who could talk with the animals
63 Book of Salvation 184
    The true meaning of the word "salvation"
64 Book of Forgiveness 187
    Balance of good and evil
65 Book of Deeds 190
    Work of Aristotle: book of numbers
66 Book of the Light Ship Athena 193
    A tour of the ship
67 Book of the Templars 198
    Secret of the Templars: intertwining flames of the inner and outer worlds
68 Book of the Holy Sepulcher 202
    Center of the birth of separateness
69 The Apple Tree 207
    Regeneration
70 The Right of Dawn 209
    The nautilus, the spiral of creation
71 Book of the Siege 212
    Planetary service of Eurocles in the transformation of Earth
72 Book of the Seven 215
    The holy force, the knowledge of balance. The seven symbols (words) given to us to understand ourselves
73 The Fall from Grace 218
    Who is man?
74 Reunion 220
    A message we leave for ourselves from another time and space
75 Book of Nations 223
    All nations that comprise Earth come from the forces of love
76 Book of Ger-Om 226
    Our Earth and its agreement

77 The Surrender to Manna 229
   Acknowledge and surrender to your God within
78 Book of Peace 231
   A message from Sananda
79 Book of the New Tomorrow 233
   Transfiguration of the Earth plane – the New Age
80 The Greatest Story Ever Told 237
   Your many senses
Index 241

Acknowledgements

I thank the "Angel Group" for listening and discussing these books as they were given. Also I give hugs and thanks to my husband, Richard, who has helped me understand the words given through me and that, indeed, the words given do make sense! And Tony Stubbs, thank you for "holding my hand" as I went through the processes of book publishing. Your expertise has been a God-send.

Foreword by Richard L. Thompson

It has been foretold as we approach what some have dubbed the End Times, significant arcane knowledge would be revealed to humanity. The Mayan calendar ends on December 21, 2012, which marks the closure of one 'world' and the commencement of a new, but unknown, next 'world.' We are rapidly approaching that date. The knowledge that has been foretold, some of which has already begun to surface, promises to challenge much of the history currently accepted as fact and the understanding of individuals as they relate to All That Is.

With respect to history, humanity seems to accept as fact any story repeated often enough. We must all remember that 'history' is only what has been recorded, and, even then through the filter and bias of the recorder or writer. Hence, the descriptive reference as 'his-story (or her-story).' Most of history has also been recorded and modified to support the point of view of the most powerful institutions, i.e., the church and the governments.

However, newly rediscovered writings are already forcing a re-examination of history and religious dogma, one example being the role of the feminine throughout time. This book is a major contribution toward the unveiling of long-hidden or intentionally obscured information. These writings offer a unique commentary on many subjects, but all of them relate to the central theme that humanity is unique and transcendent. It, as with all new knowledge, must be read with the perspective of an open mind and a loving heart. Indeed, there is something within this book for everyone. You may not resonate with each and every book within, but some are certain to connect with your spirit, heart, and mind.

We, humanity, don't even begin to grasp who we are and our place in creation. We have an existence on this planet (and others) that is far longer and more complex than has been perceived. However, more importantly, we are on the cusp of a grand new adventure, and the writings contained within this book help reveal some of where we have been and offer a glimpse into where we are headed.

As it has been said, if you want to change your life, all you need to do is change your perception of it. Ready! Set! Change!

— Richard L. Thompson, ordained minister and spiritual teacher

Preface

The following writings were written by the process of inter-dimensional communication. I was given the preamble to the books, and soon after, I started receiving the books. The books are meant to be read slowly and may take a while to process. You, the reader, may resonate with some of the books but not all. Many of the books have a scientific bent which I am slowly learning to understand.

Inter-dimensional communication is a form of "hearing," "seeing," and/or "feeling." Regarding the following "books", many of them were written in less than an hour, others took from two to three sittings. When I was most centered, with my mind chatter cleared, I wrote smoothly and quickly.

My friend and guide, Sananda, has been the one to assist me with all of the books. I thank him for his time, patience, and understanding in letting these books come forth. He interpreted some of the old and ancient writings into what I call "Bev language" with the addition of much more sophisticated language than I speak. The words in each of the books were written the way that I "heard" them, so much was written in improper English. I also received names and phrases in a foreign tongue so I spelled them as I "saw" the words or as phonetically correct as I could get.

The bold italicized words in the following books are words given by Sananda. Those words that are italicized but not bold are my own words. Following the books are questions that I had asked for clarification. The answers are from "spirit" unless they are in bold print and given to me by Sananda.

You will notice that in some of the books, I was given the location to where they can be found. Perhaps one day, many of the original books will be found.

I welcome you, the reader, to write if you understand a book and can explain it for the benefit of others. Or if you are familiar with a similar story to any of the books and I have the names slightly off, please write and share. That is what this book is all about. Sharing the history and the knowledge of the Universes will assist us in gaining the knowledge and wisdom of who and what we are, why we are here on this Earth at this time, and a glimpse into our future (which we are creating).

This book is Volume I. At this writing, I have been told that there will be a total of three volumes. The prelude to the books was written on March 12, 2002, with the 80th book (last book in this volume) written on July 19, 2004. I have noticed that many of these books were written when it was time for me, as well as others with whom I have shared these writings, to understand the depth and meaning of what was being said, like the old adage: "When the student is ready, the teacher will appear."

About the Author

Beverly J. Thompson

I started communicating (at least consciously) inter-dimensionally in the late 1990s. After years of studying and reading everything metaphysical (I had a ferocious appetite for this), I finally quieted myself and started meditating. A whole new world opened up for me and I experienced many visions.

I have three children who are now grown and on their own and a wonderful husband, Rick, who is very much in sync with me spiritually. In the early 1990s, all the children lived at home and I had a growing interior design business. Until 1993, we lived in the Chicago suburb of Glenview, Illinois. We moved to South Carolina. Deep inside of me I had felt a constant yearning to move from Illinois. Much of that yearning was fear based in that I felt the future earth changes were going to greatly affect that area. Now I know my fear was unnecessary. When my husband decided to retire from the investment financial business, we got out our copy of the I AM America map by Lori Toye and selected numerous locations where we thought we may like to live. On one occasion while looking at the map and pondering where to live, I became frustrated and anxious and decided that it was late and time for bed. I checked the children's bedrooms to make sure all was well with them and noticed my daughter, then age 8, not in her bed. She had fallen asleep on the family room sofa. I gently tried to wake her to steer her to her bedroom and she started talking in her sleep. Puzzled and interested to hear what she had to say, I decided to get into a conversation with her "asleep" self. She did not know my husband and me were looking at map for a place to live. She mumbled the word "map" which certainly got my attention. She then said very clearly and distinctly, "Look at the map in your heart". I tried to continue the conversation but to no avail. This had a profound effect on me. We moved to the south and I am sure our former neighbors thought we were a little crazy moving from a beautiful home and having high profile and well-paying careers (at least my husband did). Our lives were quite normal, living the American dream. And then we started waking up.

It was the mid 1980's when I started reading channeled (inter-dimensional communication) work. I was intrigued to learn about other beings, such as the masters and angels, and why they had such an intense interest in our planet. I remember reading about Lightworkers and wondered who these magnificent people might be, not knowing that I (and you) are one of them. I never considered myself a writer. In fact, I never was a good English student in school. After I had communicated inter-dimensionally for over a year, I realized I was to publish some of the messages I received. I now know I am considered a "scribe." I have had many holy surprise moments (I usually use another word other than "surprise"). My mouth opens, my jaw drops, and I am thinking, "Who? Me?." But I know I have volunteered to be a scribe and am greatly honored to do the work.

We are learning, no, we are remembering who and what we are. Honor ourselves as we look into a mirror and honor all others as we gaze into their eyes. Life is incredible!

Beverly is an ordained minister and is an intuitive counselor and energy therapist. She also continues with her work in commercial and residential interior design. She and her husband, Rick, publish a quarterly newsletter *"The Gathering of Angels."* Also see their web site www.thegatheringofangels.com.

The Mystery of the Universes
A Prophecy Fulfilled

On March 12, 2002, I received the following:

On stone tablets are written a Prophecy and Writings of the Mystery of the Universes. There are 12/20 such writings in each of the Twelve Tribes of Israel shall there be twenty books of knowledge. These tablets are written in the language of the Sumer.[1] *[I see a winged sphinx guarding the area of these tablets.]* They lie in the forceps of the Father.[2]

The pot is ready; it has reached its boiling point.

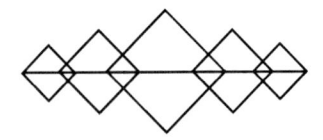

Q – What are the twelve tribes?
A – The twelve points of creation from which we exist.
Q – What does the word "forceps" refer to?
A – Bringing forth
Q – After I finished the first 80 books, I note that these books come from many places, not only on this planet, but others as well. Therefore they all were not written in the Sumer language. Was it prophesied that these writings would be made available at this time? Is it that the writings or book in and of itself is the prophecy on the tablets and not the writings themselves?
A – And now you understand.
Q – Am I a part of this boiling pot?
A – All of mankind is part of this boiling pot.

---

1 Sumer an ancient country of Mesopotamia in a region now part of southern Iraq

2 *Keys of Enoch*, Key 319:54: And the twelve vibrating pathways of the human body will be activated so completely that we will actively serve as the 12 tribes of the true spiritual Israel upon the face of the earth.

March 21, 2002

Book of Kings

I was taken to The Temple of Isis, which is located alongside the Nile River in Egypt. Next to the large temple is a small pillared temple. Sananda stood at the center of one end of the temple (toward the Nile) to energetically read the Book of Kings buried there. I merged with Sananda to receive the translation of the words.

This book shall be found during the end times of The Great Experiment. The many leaders throughout the eras have left their mark on humanity. Now is the time of the Great Tribulation. This tribulation will weigh the facts of our brethren, those who have seeded the Earth. What has mankind learned about density?

He that holds the seeds that have not been tainted shall be the first to awaken. The rulers of this galaxy, Jovàn, shall relinquish all control when the people awaken. His duties finished, he shall return onto The Great Central Sun. Those who have worked closely with Jovàn shall also return to their former stations. Any deceit from these ones shall break down in the systems of the planet Earth upon their release. The energy they held in place shall be transmuted into the black matter to be released when called upon.

The Angel of Death shall return to the left hand of Creator Source, for death (ignorance) shall be no more.

Explosions of gases shall be seen with this removal of energy. Light shall enter all darkness, all recesses that once existed on Planet Terra. May she return to her rightful state for the birth of The New Age.

The Galactic Council of Seven shall move into place those contracts written three ages back. The golden spectrum of light shall enter into all systems of life in this galaxy. It shall extend slowly into all other galaxies in this universal quadrant.

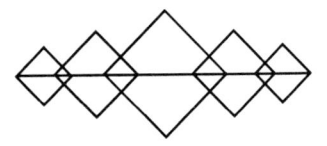

On June 30, 2002, I received the following message:

In the eternal shall you know yourself. In that state of beingness shall rise the knowledge of divine essence. There will be no questions to ask, for you shall already know the answer. Oh Creator Gods of the Universe, know that you only need to ask and it shall be given.

In this embodiment?

In all your embodiments until there is no need for questions.

The physical is just one part of existence. Your present mind cannot grasp the All. Research and development is and will continue to be a part of this existence.

The minds of great civilizations are combining to produce a new paradigm. This physical rapture[1] which is occurring shall lift mankind out of the depths of despair (hell) into worlds of beauty, light, and ecstasy. New manifestations will occur with the new thought patterns existing in the many realms. You are the masters of the Divine.

---

1 Rapture – *The Living Webster Encyclopedic Dictionary of the English Language*: A state of great delight or ecstasy; often plural - a showing of extreme joy or pleasure.

Jovàn

I came, I saw, I conquered. And now I shall release.

May 30, 2005

Jovàn is a crossing, or transference of divine knowledge. A block was put into place on and around the earth plane so the lower vibrations could be played out, then return to balance. In so far as the paradigm shift, man is entering his final stage of embodied life. That part of each of you, Jovàn, is being transmuted into a higher vibration of Love, of Creator.

You embody many, many lives simultaneously. However, you have put into place a timeline, an accountability of your various life streams. In so doing, you have created another matrix of living life. This part of living life is just another aspect of you. Now you have determined that this life stream is to develop into a more realized body of divine energy. The energy is changing because you have decreed it so. This is the basis for Jovàn, the removal of the "old" to make room for the new.

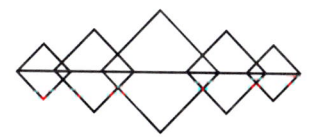

Q – Explain what is The Great Central Sun.

A – The Great Central Sun is a place/energy where all Creator energies originate. It is a part of you (the divine spirit in you) yet is comprised of twelve dimensions, each having twelve planes of existence.

Q – Is it located in any section of the Omniverse?

A – It is also the Omniverse.

Q – Could you give us a clearer understanding of our Great Central Sun?

A – There are universes within universes. This universe which you and your planet Earth are part of is composed of twelve major dimensions or rates of energy (velocity of electrons, protons, neutrons in an atom). Within each dimension are planes of existence. These planes overlap one another. Most of your human's consciousness is aware of one plane within one dimension yet you travel to other planes and dimensions. You are aware of these other planes and dimensions in your sleep and meditations. You travel these planes at your own will. You hold that power yet most humans do not remember how to use this power.

Q – What is the Galactic Council of Seven?

A – The Galactic Council of Seven is an organized intergalactic council whose responsibility includes the removal of discordant energy into a mass of realized divine love.

This council stretches over many galaxies and planes of existence. They formed to be able to penetrate the various levels of creation. They now focus on this earth and her peoples to help bring an ending to the discord that was created on this earth by the beings who think of themselves as the superior force of God/Creator. They indeed are a part of Creator, but by no means are they superior. Within creation there is no inferior or superior, there just is – creation.

---

* *Keys of Enoch*, Key 102: "The Creative Mind as the Center of this Universe is known as "Lord," "King," and "Redeemer." Note the name of this book is "Book of Kings."

January 11, 2004

The Grand Force

The grand journey of becoming our higher selves is grand in only that God is saying that all life can exist simultaneously to reach a pinnacle, and that man is truly an instrument of the All. Man can reproduce all effects of life in all areas of evolution. He is destined for the kinmanship of the worlds. There exists a multitude of worlds that are harbingers of new life. This Earth is one such place. In this book is revealed the powers bestowed upon all people of this planet. Please regard this with utmost patience and reverence. Peace in all beings.

I AM the force of Love. I AM all matter, all existence. I AM the particles of the nucleus of all living cells. I AM life.

Know Me with the gratitude that all existence is only a portion of my being. My love is my total vibration. I sing the songs of songs. The feel, the touch, the sounds are Me. I Am all worlds.

You who read these words, feel of Me. Know that you are a part of Me. As a part of Me, you have the same love within you. You have the same powers within you. Yet yield your powers until you can stand in your holy presence and know of your capabilities. Breathe in the power of love, that total ecstasy of being whole, infinite. Breathe out your love into your world. Watch this love rise up in all men. The umbrella shall lift when the light quotient reaches the signature praises of one for another. Man, know you and what you are. Know that you can reach into the heavens and form new worlds. You can form new ways of life, new beings of life. It is all creation. Creation never stops. It pulses on and on. Each of your pulses brings on new life. It is you creating and creating.

Each of you, bring your lights to the forefront. Trust your infinite ways. Wear your lights upon this beautiful jewel. She shines as an emerald in the darkened skies. The skies shall become light with your hearts open and ready to receive the holy praise. With your combined lights shall you light the way for those who cannot see, who cannot know themselves. Life is beautiful. Live it with utmost care and gratitude. You will see that all worlds will collide into One bright light. That holy time is coming. The chorus is ready to sing the praises of such an event. Walk with the knowledge that you are all divine. I cannot be without you and you cannot be without Me, for we are one and the same.

When you are able to know that truly you are the divine, create in gladness. Watch your beauty unfold as each of you puts in your pieces of life. Fear has kept you in the dark, and darkness cannot be when your lights are shining brightly. You can reach across the cosmos and hop onto every star. You can create new stars and new life. Just dream a new song and it is done. It is easy but with only the purest of hearts. You are the magnificent, the beings that can bring lives into focus for the continuation of life.

Look upon the cross and see that it is only you and your creation. You each are points of light that make up a mighty force. Grand you are in that your light shines on its own and is but a speck in the larger light of All. I Am That I Am. There can be no less and no more. I Am all eternity. There is no other force than myself. I know only of love, and that love beams into all life, all cells, all particles that make up all creation. It is the light spectrum. It is the music, the sounds, the vibrations of all in the making.

Holy ones of this Earth, use your light to bring a focus of love to take this planet into another place and time. Wise ones of old, take your positions and be ready when the final trumpet has sounded. You will hear the chorus as it sounds its tone into a new level of love and understanding. You have been the caretakers of this fine jewel and it is her time to expand into the higher heavens. Hear the bells, see the fiery light, and know that you are the life, the will of love making your choice in the continuation of new life. Each of you, sound your trumpets. Sound them loudly and joyously. Then in your silence know that I Am God.

August 9, 2002

Book of the Records

Sananda and I stand on a rock in the Atlantic Ocean, in the turquoise waters of the Baha Peninsula, land southeast of Florida near the Bahama Islands. There is a rock that juts out of the sea similar to those found in the Grand Canyon. This rock looks to be made of black lava. There is vegetation and white sand on this island. Inside this rock is a cave that holds a written record of the following:

Masters and Mistresses of the Universe,

It is with great love that we leave you with this message as it is encoded and embedded in the rocks to be found at the time of great tribulation. It will be a time when man has found the need to adapt to a new way of being, a new way of living. Throughout the ages on this beautiful planet, many have come and gone, yet left their mark on this jewel. These journeys (adventures) have been kept within the hemispheres of the planet to be retrieved when adjustments need to be made. Man needs to understand where he has been, and understand why he has lived in the manner of his ancestors that was left at his disposal.

This rock, this jewel was positioned within this solar system and galaxy to obtain knowledge of the nether. The "nether" is potential that hasn't been used to the fullest abilities that the gods had given. This arrangement was first conceived by the holy ones of the stars of the nebulae. This new system is still in its infancy, waiting for the tide to turn so mankind can again understand the great cosmos of creation.

The ages, the records, have been kept within the ethers of the planet. They may be accessed any time, any place upon the planet, as well as within the entire cosmos of creation. Within the stratum of this planet lies a layer of dense energy that binds itself to the planet. This Book of Knowledge is for all to read, to relive the history and the life of ages drawn into the magnetic bands. Access into these magnetic bands involves the power of thought combined with the divine intent of understanding to gain wisdom. Once this level of the magnetic mind is achieved does the initiate have access to these codes. There is a process that can be followed, and that process is going into that place of total submission to Creator. The body must be in total balance to resonate to the divine energies to retrieve or relive the information of life that is stored.

The greatness of this planet is its ability to break forth the energies of salvation. From the heart of Infinite Spirit shall rise the center of the Great Central Sun in its development of energy into matter. This, in and of itself, is creation in its purest form. The seed of many civilizations are brought together for the making of a new species that has the capacity to master the forces of all living essences, which become a mirror of divine experiences made manifest into the living ark of humanity. From the greatness that is being made possible shall man in his most empirical form rise into the consciousness that has been brought forth. The curtain shall be pulled to reveal this aspect of Creator Source, using infinite wisdom that has been gained to bring a new form of creation. The sound of the many universes calls out in its majesty to collect the knowledge put into the Earth Mother to understand creation in its simplest form.

The gods have made their list of those beings who shall become as them in the flesh. They shall lie down in the bowels of eternal love, bound to the forces that made them. The eternalness of love shall wind itself into a ball of white energy. Replication shall be a product of this love, so to whosoever asks shall this knowledge be available in the electromagnetic waves that surrounds and embodies the sphere.

Mathematics holds a key to understanding this tightly held knowledge. But whosoever shall witness the divine plan in its purest form shall unlock all knowledge. Let it be known to all who resides in these thoughts shall the kingdom of Heaven be revealed. The secrets of this key are in every living organism. Through the numbers of the heart, 6-8-3, shall the first door be unlocked. Osiris, the one of teleo-ography, had commissioned the set-up of civilizations through the use of biocomputations. In the Order of Melchizedek are listed the lines of communications in the opening of the Records. These are listed in geometric forms. Look into thine eye and you will have the second door opened. From there you shall find the library that is in continuous manifestation.

The Records are humanity in the making. By divine will, it is so.

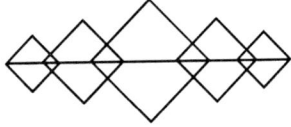

The Tablets of Time

These tablets are near to the tablets of the above writings. However, these tablets were separated and are to be found under the seas, about 50 kilometers south or southwest of the cave. There is a ridge that can be seen very clearly from the air. The waters are not deep in this area.

I note that what is scribed on these tablets appears very scientific. I see a circle with a short line at both the top and the bottom. Also I see writing that looks like a lower case "e." My vision continues, see the drawing below:

The Tablets of Time

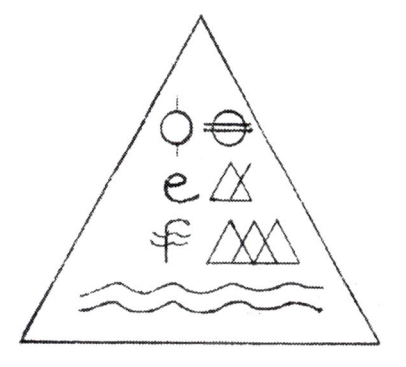

Q – What are the energies of salvation?

A - What this means is that the earth has the ability to house the many forms of life that are to be nurtured and then sent forth to create new forms of life.

Q – What are biocomputations?

A – Biology of light (sacred geometry) that makes up physical life.

Q – Explain teleo-ography.

A – Communication through the senses.

Q – Is this book the same as the Akashic Records?

A – What you term "Akashic Records" is indeed the records we speak of in this book. However, the Akashic Records are the records of all life in all time periods traversing the different dimensions.

Q – Again, are they not one and the same?

A – The Akashic Records include man and his works. This Book of Records includes man's creations and his being created.

Q – Is this book what will be found as "the Hall of Records"?

A – The Hall of Records you ask about is a list of energies, logistically located on and about the earth. They are records of time caplets, signatures of the various creations of this planetary structure. They serve as a focus for interplanetary communications.

November 12, 2002

Book of the Ages I

In ages past, the mysteries of mankind were being revealed through the work of the Soltecs. These wonderful beings masked themselves as they became of the human to establish a new way of being in the density of matter that was to become the way for the next five thousand years. The men and women of the Soltecs gave of themselves in establishing the teachings of the Essenes, the inner way to the Godhead of Creation. My life as Yeshua ben Josef followed those teachings. They were given to me when I was a young boy. I understood them to be the truth and never wavered from the totality of the spirit they embraced. Philosophies of the Bruins also embrace these concepts. The Bruins can be found in the lower European countries.

This book was recorded two thousand years after the Soltec's inception (three thousand years before my birth as Yeshua). The transcripts are still hidden in the caves of Madagascar. They shall be found in or near the Year of the Dove, 2010.

In the beginning was the word. The sound went out, and as it went out, it built upon itself. As it built upon itself, it took a form. As it took form, the sounds intensified to a crescendo of utmost brilliance. The Master, the Energy of the Godhead, breathed out the energy of Creation into form. This mastery of form is in All, for All would not exist without this outbreath.

Within this All is Creation in forms with intelligence. These forms of intelligence shall create other forms as an expression of Creation. This intense energy shall reach out and become the Heavens. The heavens of manifestation shall be the Ones of brilliance. These great Lights shall divide and make many of themselves. They shall be as Ones who create within their own creation. As ones of divided creation, they shall act as many for the whole of the One. From the finite into the infinite shall all manifestations exist.

This is the first of a series of the Most High, writings from the Godhead of Creation. It Is, It Shall Be, therefore It Is So.

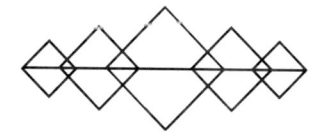

Q – Would you please explain more about the Soltecs?

A – The Soltecs live mostly in the fifth dimension because of their preference to maintain a physical body. However, they also go into spirit form through the seventh dimension. They "rule" the cosmos or this portion of it in that they have the ability to voice out their light creations.

They humbly decided to concentrate their energies to this Earth because of the denseness this planet had become.

Q – Are they known by other names?

A – Elohim, Nimion, Wayshowers are names you may recognize.

Q – Who are the Bruins?

A – A dark-skinned race of man who have dwindled in population on this Earth. They once were great seafarers.

April 6, 2003

Book of the Ages II

The eternal quest for knowledge on the earth plane stands to reason why man is always in pursuit of further understandings of the workings of life and the universe. An understanding of all life in its myriad forms will be achieved through the navigation of the heart-mind into micro-macrocosms of the basics of life form. This book explores the inner reaches and the outer reaches of the basic element of light, the substance of all life.

Light can be summed up in two ways: (1)- the pineal copular resonance factor, and (2)- the arrangement of diodes. The orchestration of light is manifested by the use of the mind energy. The mind energy is also light, so one can say that light begets light. A further illustration of this is in seeing the atmospheric changes of the skies. Lightning is produced by the polarities of the ions. The colder air has ions with a higher negative magnetic while the warmer air has a higher positive magnetic. When these forces meet, they mesh into a large spark of energy which grounds itself in the earth. Thus the energies merge, which produces a higher energy voltage. The earth is the catalyst while the air is the factor. But what caused this air flow?

All movement starts with the heart. The mind moves the energy into a position, an outward manifestation. When the many manifestations that exist on the earth plane mingle, they cause the energies to flow out into a circular pattern. Depending upon the energies released, the atmosphere around the earth heats up or cools off. These energies meet and can cause the storms, a high-powered electrical exchange. Therefore you have two energies meeting, which causes a massive reaction or action.

The energies that exist in the body are part of a much larger energy, the God force. Each individual on the earth plane can use this God force in whatever way he or she wants. This is a free-will planet. An idea or spark starts in the heart area, the mind which includes the brain and the three major glands – pineal, hypothalamus, and the pituitary – goes into action and sorts out the message received. The mind will act and put the energy into motion. Through the body's sensory receptors, one receives the energy released by another. This energy is in constant flow and can be changed or transmuted through the heart/mind. Creation continues with this process. The human chooses what he or she wants to experience. The energy is worked within the total system, which is termed "god."

The earth's movements act from the heart of the Mother. The heart, also a part of the God force, is greatly affected by the energies released by all who inhabit her body. Her spirit closely mirrors that of the other star systems that resonate at a similar frequency. She is part of the dance that includes all of the cosmos. All of the cosmos is linked through the energy wave patterns yet the wave patterns resonate at different frequencies (dimensions), which gives the appearance of separateness.

This universe of light is the smallest particum to the whole of the dimensions combined. It is the whole and absolute. It moves, it changes form, but the energies remain constant. Life can then be summed up by this truth: All matter is an arrangement of light. In the earth realm, the various arrangements of light are called the ages.

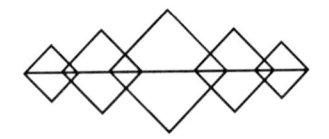

When you contemplate the ocean, you see the ebb and flow. The waves get larger because of an action on or in the earth. You notice a change in the ebb and flow yet the particles that make up the waters remain much the same. So it is with God, that wonderful force that makes up who and what we are. Life continues and will never cease to end. That cannot be. Therefore love life in the moment. You are the creators. Create wisely.

This book was given to the Essenes. These ideas were central to their (the Essenes) thought.

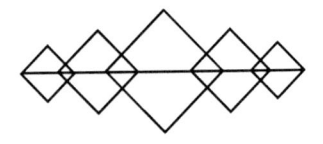

Q – *What is the pineal copular resonance factor?*
A – Sound

Pineal: (1) – resembling the shape of a pine cone; (2) – Anatomy: pertaining to the pineal gland. It is aware of daylight, which influences a body's awareness to time. The pineal gland acts as the portal through which the realms of energy and light enter the physical and material bodies. Through this portal, these light transmissions are mediated into the physical bloodstream as hormones. These hormones regulate the energy distribution and functioning of the physical body.

Copular: (1) – something that links together; (2) – Anatomy: a connecting bone or cartilage.

Resonance: vibration.

Diode: type of electron tube which has an anode (positive pole) and a cathode (negative pole).

November 24, 2002

Book of the Song

Are we with the Essenes?

Indeed, we are. We have come to a spot where the information from the Living Light was given. The Essenes were a people that communicated with fifth to the seventh dimensional beings. They could travel the stars but their mission was to be the earth, our Lady Gaia. Lady Gaia called out in the name of the Light. Many beings answered her call. Thus information was given to the Essenes in the name of Golden Peace. Their books hold the truth.

Whispering sounds filled the universe. In the quietness of Creator came a primordial call. The call went out, simply went out. A chorus ensued as the sound continued. Lights of many colors were the effects of the sounds, for they were one. Because there was no one to witness this sound, the sound continued until it became a cohesion of vibrations. The cohesion of vibrations became form, each form consisting of the same vibrations or color. The colors intermingled into a moving form of exquisite beauty, turning and twisting and flowing as the sounds continued. Each vibration and color knew of itself, therefore each also knew of the other vibrations in which they were entwined.

As the vibrations continued, the forms grew in their beauty and intensity. The vibrations/colors formed themselves into various shapes. Each shape knew of itself and could create from itself. All of creation is the chorus.

Within all of creation, listen and you will be able to hear your own particular song. Listen to the other songs. The word is sound; the sound is color; the color is creation. Beautiful one of the Universe, the chorus sings of my magnitude. I create it so and so it is.

November 24, 2002

Book of Alignment

The teachings of the Essenes continue:

It is here where we learn the processes of integration. We integrate the colors and sounds of Creator in order to become creators ourselves. The process is quite simple yet in the density of the human, it is a concept that is difficult to imagine. Yet while in the process, is quite easy to apply in each of your lives. My teachings as Yeshua strongly supported this way, this truth, this light.

Be as the river that flows ever so gently through you. It touches the very rocks that steer its course. As it passes over and around the rocks, you pick up the essence of each rock. And so it is the creation of creation.

In the moment, all exists. All exists as One and each part completes the Whole. The essence of All, and All that will ever be, is here now, in this moment. To cast out is the outer of creation. It maintains that of the whole yet has its own ability to cast out again. Cast yourselves out into the wilderness and make of My creation whatever you can dream, think, feel, imagine. The wonders of creation live within each one of you. You are the composite of the All, so nothing is lost. That is not possible. Play your parts. Look out into all and the heavens shall manifest themselves to you. Love the creation just as I love you. There can be no other way.

The magnificence of Creator is your ability to create. Be this with all the sounds and colors that make up Me (and you). Feel the colors as they work through you. You have the capability to move them into any shape that you wish. What wonders do We create.

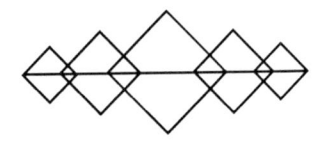

Q – The name of this book is Alignment. Does this mean we are aligned with Creator in creating?

A – Align yourselves in creating out of love. You were all created out of love of the Creator. When you know there is no creation that isn't love, then creation without love is not possible.

Q – On this Earth plane, it appears that much of life is without love.

A – All, everything is with love. Lessons are learned when it appears that a life has no love. You have many lives and experiences within each life stream. You created your life streams to truly learn love. When in an embodiment, you may have felt very little love from your fellow man and family.

Q – What about the entities that we call aliens. I have read that many of them do not have the capacity of emotions we have. Please explain their basic mission.

A – Without going into the many, many types of life, yes there are human type entities that have very little emotion. You ask, how can they love without emotion?

There are entities that act as "robots." They are trained for specific tasks and have great technologies. However, they cannot grasp the amount of energy that the human holds. They can traverse the lower dimensions with their advanced technologies but cannot break the barriers of the higher dimension (fifth and up) because they are unable to hold the vibration necessary to be in that space. Whereas the human has that ability to raise again their vibration to live in that Christed state. The only way to live in that Christed state is love, all freedom from any fear you may now experience. Just as Jeshua said, "It is the way, the truth, and the light." The way is alignment with Creator; the truth is that love is the only way, and the light is the spirit of God Creator.

December 1, 2002

Book of Genesis

Continued writings from the Essenes...

Yes, there is a Book in your Bible that is the same name. The Book in your Bible was gleaned from these teachings. Know that all truth resides in your perceptions. However, keep in mind that your perceptions are being shaken to bring in the higher teachings and knowledge of this universe. Many ones have called forth in their interpretations of what is. Please keep an open mind and heart as you read these words. The truth of this universe and all universes shall set you free, free from limitation.

Bound by the unlimitedness of the Creator, we bring these truths of the divine flow of energy power to this plane of existence. This plane shall be called The Division of Oneness. All shall be as One yet have their own capacities for creating their own manifestations from the elixir of light that shall pass through all creation. Energy in the form of passive existence shall be stimulated into a compound of frequencies that provoke it into form by the use of divine thought. Manifestations shall be of the highest form of creative power.

The star matrix- two intersecting four-sided pyramids- is the means of transportation of form from one dimension into another. The dimensions are always accessible to all manifestation yet in the dimensions that are seen and felt in the plane of Earth, those in the lower vibrational forms cannot access those in the higher forms without full focus and concentration to integrate the higher vibratory rates. This gives man the will to produce within his own sphere.

The star- the mode of dimensional transportation- is the secret to opening the lower dimensional matrix to intertwine into the higher realms of existence. The access code is formed from the denominator[1] of the first frequency in the spectrum of light combined with the frequency of the fourth spectrum. Thus you have the color which predominates the dimensional intersections. From the realms of the most high are the lower realms made manifest. This gives the higher realms the opportunity to understand the power that they are. Given the choice of free will to these inhabitants of Earth, these beings in the higher realms shall know of their power. It is a choice for all to participate in the game.

From the stars located in the seventh heaven will the stars of the other four heavens be able to manifest their choices in this free-will planet. The matrix of open manifestation has now been set upon this body who gives her love in this experiment. This is a game of total love in the formation of new manifestation made possible by the love of Creator God. All has been made in the likeness of Creator in the light frequencies that have been provided. The song is being sung. Hear O Gods that whosoever should manifest upon this jewel, shall feel the love that bestows from the Sun/Son the magnificence of all creation.

It has been spoken.

---

1. Denominator – *The Living Webster Encyclopedic Dictionary of the English Language:* That term of a fraction, usually written under the line, which indicates its denomination, or shows the number of equal parts into which the unit is divided.
2. This body refers to this earth.

**Star Matrix
or Merkaba**

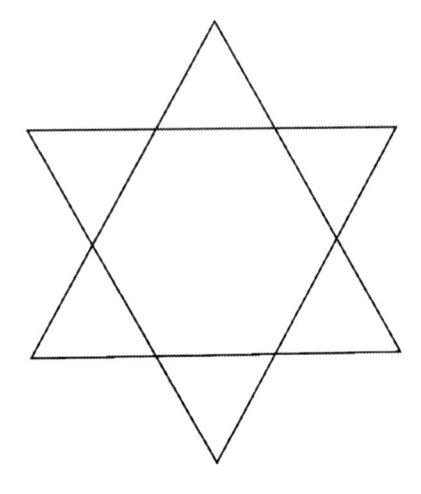

Q – What is meant by the star matrix?

A – The star matrix is also called the merkaba. This mode of interdimensional transportation will become common knowledge with open use once this world has awakened in its fullness. The merkaba is the main mode of interdimensional transportation due to its structure that can resonate with the various levels of dimensions. Once the human's mind can grasp the concept that such a thing is part of us all, then it will become easier to rotate the fields, hence move in the merkaba.

See "The Keys of Enoch," Key 301, which further explains this star matrix or merkaba.

Q – What is seventh heaven?

A – Seven dimensions.

Q – What is meant by the "the other four heavens"?

A – Those planets that exist in the first four dimensions.

October 2002

⊚ 9

Book of Winter

We are in the area of the Alps. We stand before the King of the Rocks who lives among the people of Jezbel. Their story tells us of the time that the Earth was forming into the density of the Third Age, the age of evolution in its infancy. This book reminds us of our actions when they were in alignment with the Sun God. These writings depict the enormous aptitude of the beings who came to Earth to plant the seeds of deliverance into the world of form. Their story is written in the rocks upon the hills of Northern Italy in the area of Sanspeii.

We, the Elders, bring forth the truth of this day to impart the knowledge of the One that transforms the form into dense matter of a frequency of manna. To this we salute those who will come and volunteer themselves in the evolution of the form into the density of this new star that shall deliver unto the Whole a newness, an intelligence of form that shall be the forerunner of new civilizations.

The plan is one that supports the divine will of Creator in the auspices of energized form. Form shall take on many faces. The systems of Orion, Pleiades, Antares, and Arcturus shall be the first to compose their efforts into the manifestation of the many forms that are to dwell upon the Earth, this Lady whom we so lovingly call "our Divine Keeper." Into her recesses shall the energies of creation be positioned for their retrieval to support life upon and inside her surface. To each of the planetary systems that are a part of this manifestation, we salute you. Those ones of Sirius, come forth in your intelligence to bring with you the divine laws of manifestation of the physical. Place your hearts into the pool of divine coordination that these four planetary systems are providing. From this union will the forms of all life spring forth into a network of life supporting life. All manner of manifestation shall be brought forth by the elements of the body of Earth, until such time or energy vibration that will support life beyond this sphere.

Travel between systems shall continue as this learning and creation process unfolds itself into myriad visions becoming denser forms. Manna shall be broken down into elements of life forms which shall include the following: the hu-man body with open intelligence of co-creative process, horticulture to support hu-man and animal, and animal to support their own intelligence as well as support man in his endeavors. In support of the horticultural systems shall these ones be able to bring in their representations of the insect systems to assist in the reproduction of the plant system. This process shall be woven into a circle of life represented by our mark of the triangle with the circle. The eye of creation shall be the center of this triangle to denote the presence of the divine. All creation shall go through the eye.

The mineral kingdom shall be the support of the energies of this manifestation. These minerals shall become as the makeup of Our Divine Keeper. Our Lady shall have the authority to move within her skin those elements that support her well being should any distortion be made from those manna occupying her body.

A new day is rising upon the shoulders of this Universe. We leave these writings within the confines of Our Lady so that communication shall continue among our planetary systems.

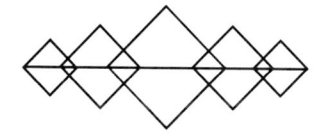

The eye represents the Intergalactic Command of the Seven Sisters. The Seven Sisters represents more than the Pleiades.

Q – Why is this book called "Book of Winter"?

A – Winter denotes a stillness before plant life springs from its sleep in your spring time. Also there is less light from your sun in the winter months, so it is like a sleeping, a darkness with the return of the light.

This book talks about a new creation, thus a new light being brought to this planet. Many, many beings presently incarnated on this planet are originally from the four planetary systems listed in the book – Orion, Pleiades, Antares, and Arcturus. Your whales and dolphins as well as some humans come from Sirius.

January 25, 2003

Book of Memory

The time of the Vascerealiation was beginning to take root on this planet. Beings from the star ship Acillia transported their knowledge of the stars that inhabit the star system Andromeda to this plane of existence. These beings held the code of cross transfiguration of the humanoid species. Their input into the man becoming hu-man is written and stored in the vaults of the higher dimensions. This book can be accessed through the channel of the fourth ray of the seventh sun.

Please explain what is the "fourth ray of the seventh sun."

The fourth ray is the color green which occupies your heart chakra. The seventh sun is the living life of the seventh dimension. Many of the soul groups now incarnate upon planet Earth are part of this dimension where their higher selves reside. Memories may awaken as these soul groups read these words.

Massive coordination of the systems that reside in the quadrant of this universe shall awaken to their roles placed within them of their knowledge of their voluntary participation of the species of man being injected with the data from the Great Central Sun. This infusion of energies shall make man into the image of the All. All systems that are available for an increase in the making of a species whose power is to combine the legacies of the various groups of beings created by and for the combination of said systems shall result in the magnificents of the magnificence. All systems shall have their say in the development of the new species. The combinations made manifest shall be their own government. All of their resources shall be within, and they shall have the knowledge of their respective stars within their structures. Thus all creation from these beings shall be made of the All of creation.

They shall make their own ways, their own means, their own lives without the interference of any one group. This means that these hu-mans shall be protected by their own makings. Decisions of how these hu-mans are to interface with other species shall be of their own choosing. With this experiment shall the various forces of the universe unite in their own development.

Night shall become day and day shall become night. These two forces shall intertwine in the making of a new understanding for the All. The void shall be used to pull out the living light to manifest in the physical biology of the seven lower dimensions. There exists nothing within the void, yet All is there to be molded into the making of reality, of various realities.

We, the Brotherhood of Creative Forces, begin a new day and new night of a new type of life form to start the new way of being. The memory of All shall be locked within the structures so that this energy can be molded into a new pattern of existence. We stand by our declaration that we assist in this making yet recede in our governance. We will this so, and so it is.

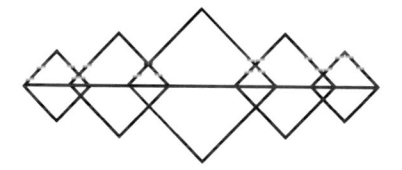

Q – Why is human spelled with a hyphen?

A – Hu-man: Hu is a Sanskrit word for God or divine. Man is the physical body.

Q – What is vascerealiation?

A – An antithesis *(opposition)* of the anatomy changing into a new form which can hold more information within its cells.

Q – How many systems made themselves available for an "increase" in the making of a species?

A – Over 188,000 volunteered their expertise in this new human.

Q – Please explain what is meant by an "increase"?

A –An increase in the capabilities of man to hold the higher divinitic energies.

Q - Is part of this book saying man has free-will?

A – Yes.

Q – Who is the Brotherhood of Creative Forces?

A – The 188,000 who volunteered their expertise.

January 9, 2003

Book of Wonders

Deep within the caverns of ancient Egypt are written the philosophies of the ancients, the ones who existed on this plane before the return of the star people of the Ana conda. These people left their greatness of passive evolution to be explored and built upon by the beings that were to next inhabit this planet. Their points of evolution are as follows:

Energy, those beams of light sparked by the command of the rays of the sixteenth galaxy of the Andromedans, shall burst forth on this wonderful sphere to bring in the forces of love expressed in the division of the colors worn by the adepts of The Great Central Sun. In the evolution of the forces of two commingling in an arc, shall rise the archetype of the new being that shall exist within the matter of the sphere of new origins.

With the combination of the seventh ray of violet and the fourth ray of green, protons will spin and split into two opposing forces. This repulsion will break open the seed of the original coalesced form of the living liquid light and spill into a new seed, an expanded light form. The light form shall form into two groups of beings, one a genderless form of humanoid who will be the springboard of action into the physical body, and the second group, beings that shall be the ones of science of biological genetics. This second group shall be the ones that open the purest form of man made in the image or love energies of Creator Source. This God form shall process their God forms and make holy their creations. With the help of the first group, will the form become a part of the living Earth. The body shall be made of the elements of Great Terra. With her greatness shall this new form move into levels of manifestation that will be as guides to future planets and civilizations.

All biological form will be built upon the foundation of the seven rays and maintain their biological knowledge throughout their evolutionary changes. All knowledge will be coded within every cell structure and every atom, so nothing will ever be forgotten. Love of Creator will live within All and know of its greatness through all beings. Eternity is and all life exists with the moment. All moments shall stretch into waves of electrical currents pulsing within the liquid light. Spheres of consciousness shall result, all connected by the magnetic frequencies pulsed from The Great Central Sun.

Life in this region of this great wave of planetary stars shall become a focus for biological life of the form that has the capacity to become the master of Evolution. Focused intent from ones of the planetary systems of Arcturus, Andromeda, Sirius, and the Pleiades shall assist this process. This form shall be the wonder of the universes in their development, their makeup of creation, and their ability to create. We bring this knowledge forth to be remembered. Nothing can stop this process and may the wonders of Evolution begin.

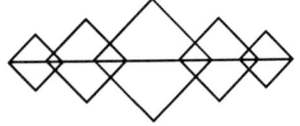

Q – Please explain "living liquid light."
A – Living liquid light is the divine energy of the Godhead, the Great Central Sun.

Q – In other books such as "Book of Winter," the planetary systems of Orion, Pleiades, Antares, and Arcturus were the first to compose their efforts in the making of the many earth forms. This book speaks of Arcturus, Andromeda, Sirius, and the Pleiades as the ones who have assisted the process of biological life on this planet.

A – Each has their own specialties with some of the specialties overlapping:

- Orion – genetics through the code of Universal Laws.
- Pleiades – emotional behavior.
- Antares – use of light in the process of evolving forms.
- Arcturus – biological codes within the spectrum of stretched time lines (time lines - wave lengths of the seven rays).
- Andromeda – the use of sound/light and the ability to mold it into the coalesced form.
- Sirius – ability to maintain the higher frequencies without the breaking of these higher frequencies when used to mold the lower physical forms.

February 3, 2003

Book of Tomorrow

Tomorrow means a new day. Within this context you may surmise that you will begin a new day within your lifetime. Every day is a new day with your actions and reactions, observations, and relationships. This book is about looking (perceiving) what tomorrow really means, how it is made or manifested. The clock ticks, so let us move with this pulsing of the clock.

Within the matrix of the web of creation are the many possibilities that exist for a new day or a new time. What tomorrow brings is totally up to the creators. In order to create, we must be able to perceive. In order to perceive, we must be able to transcend memory and build upon knowledge that has been built in the web of evolution.

The web moves into a new zone, one that is tangible in the physical. Since humankind will continue in the physical through the seven dimensions, new webs are being built to accommodate new thoughts. Memory of what has been will be contained in the similitude of the horizon effect. The sun rises on the horizon, bringing new life with every ray that is beamed to this time and this space. It simply resonates to the beat of the pulse of Prime Creator. The spectrum that is displayed is absorbed into the particles of the life that exist on this plane. With each new day or rotation of the planet is a new day to expand Creator in the physical. With the mind of the human shall the mind of God grow in its magnificence.

Thus all minds of the universes grow with every breath that is taken.

Tomorrow is just a new step into worlds of fantasy made manifest. The thoughts of the humans control their existence on the beautiful planet of Terra. Knowledge of the stars relate to Terra in that she has a body that is to be nourished. Each planet and star create in their own way to the whole of creation.

Source shall be used within itself to realize that time and space are but an illusion, an illusion that holds the threads of new life.

We, the beings of Akhtum, acknowledge the thoughts of Creator in the manifestation of the physical on this wonderful body of Terra. May tomorrow live to continue this creative process.

Q - Where can this book be found?

A – These beings landed on earth and were here to leave their thoughts in this matrix of humanity. This book can be found in the physical within the writings of Abraham.

February 6, 2003

Book of Eternal Life

During the times of Atlantis, people were asking about all their lives for they had the technology to bring into focus each of their lives. Because of this, we shared on the inner realms the technology that is required to view one's many lives in this space and time as well as all other spaces and times in which each and all have lived or had consciousness.

This line of thinking is difficult to explain because of the limited knowledge that man of Earth has at this moment.

Life is and ever shall be. Life is the total of all existence and all existence is life. Manifest with thoughts all existence. Form and shape are the results of thoughts. We live within Creator. There is no existence outside of Creator – there is no outside.

Because of all being within the Creator, then all life can be accessed. Time exists within the confines of space. So to traverse space, traverse through time. Time can be slowed, accelerated or stopped. Because of this, then all space can be traveled. With the use of Creator in its most minute form, these particles of light can be brought into focus. Focus with intent our existences. The sense of feeling can put one in touch with other life forms, other lives in this planetary system as well as all others. You can face yourselves in all forms and understand what creation is all about.

To do this, focus your thought on a whirlwind/spiral "cloud." As it spins, focus your intent on any one aspect of Creator. Form shall gather as you remain totally focused on this manifestation. All particles will come into place and you will see or sense your creation. Take this information into yourselves and you will see the other parts of yourself. You will know your former and future lives. You will witness others' creations as they intertwine with your creations. You will witness the intersecting and interlocking of all creation. With this understanding and knowledge, you will know that all existence is the thoughts of Creator in which you are all a part.

This life on this beloved planet is for existence of Creator to experience itself in a form that co-creates with itself. Because of this experience all life forms shall be able to conduct themselves in the total life support system that is to manifest throughout all of creation.

This book is from you to yourself. The patterns of manifestation are within Creator and you are the creators of the patterns. We leave this book to be read upon the awakening period. We are your future selves.

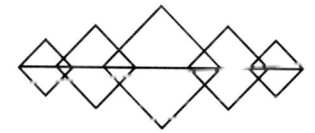

Q – This book says that we can access our other lives by focusing on any one aspect of Creator. Please give an example of an "aspect" of Creator.

A – Suppose you want to know why you may have a phobia in this life. Let's say you are claustrophobic (morbid fear of narrow spaces or closed rooms). With full intent, concentrate your wanting to find out why you have this condition. Suddenly you will reconnect with a lifetime where fear came over you through the acts of man or perhaps you may have drowned. Once you relive this fearful episode, concentrate on what happened next in that life. Perhaps you left your body and found yourself in another world. You will find that the drowning incident or death of that life just moved you to another place, a beautiful peaceful place. Therefore you release that fear and your present day condition of claustrophobia.

Obviously, you can focus on happier lifetimes. It does not matter as all experiences make up you and Creator.

February 9, 2003

⓮

Book of Myopia[1]

First the electron, then the proton. With the balance of the yin/yang will man rediscover his roots and his future.

The discovery of balance, man searching for his infinite wisdom, shall manifest upon the earth in the times of tribulation. Discovery of the eternalness of man and of life shall be realized by all humanity.

In the sacred searches upon the planet shall be found not only this book but many other books that extol knowledge of the Infinite Creator. Man shall turn his eye inward to glimpse the glory of his being. He shall recognize the palate that he has laid out in his quest for the divine truth of All That Is. He shall find that all truth lies within, the perceptions of truth varying among the masses.

Any misconceptions shall be apparent to those who truly understand what reality really is. Is it our own flesh and blood? Yes. Is it the planet and the stars? Yes. Is it the knowledge of God? Yes. Is it the physical that we can see, touch, taste, hear, and smell? Yes. Is it the love of Creator? Yes.

It is all of these because all of these are your own creations. Humanity in its quest to understand Creator shall use

---

[1] Myopia: *The Living Webster Encyclopedia Dictionary* – a condition of the eye in which images are focused in front of the retina, objects being seen distinctly only when near to the eyes, nearsightedness; lack of foresight.

their eyes to remember their roots. Life shall open to include everything. In the days of old when the earth was just an embryo, we said "Let there be light" and there was light. Light has manifested upon this beautiful planet to nourish itself and the many life forms that needed a planet to call home. Forms are to be utilized for the Creator to know of itself.

Life is and ever shall be. Seeds have been planted in this realm of the eternal. Each shall find their way, their way of being.

I Am that I AM. I AM God in all forms.

Book of Eternal Life
from the Pharaohs of Avalon

In the celebrations that are to follow this divine plan of ascension, man will be asking more about eternity. What does this mean, what are the consequences, and where are we going? This book will answer these questions and more. These are taken from the writings of the Pharaohs of Avalon.

Into the night with the twinkling of stars comes the thought: "What are we?" What are the stars, what are the heavens? I feel so beckoned by the outreach of the heavens. I feel them enfolding me, the warmth of their arms reaching around me to hold me in their presence. I feel one with them yet somehow separate. What is this? What is this earth below my feet? What is this life that grows on and below this earthly surface? Aw, so many questions my heart wants answered.

To this questioning I leave my heart open to receive the light, the internal light of God and the Goddess.

The crowning glory of all civilizations comes at that moment that all questioning comes to an end. You know that life is an open-ended existence. You may crave a lifetime of total silence or one of total dominion over your fellow man. You are all of these and more. The body of the Christ is among the living. It lives in each and every one of mankind, and the trees, the soil, the rocks, the waters. It is the soul of all encompassed in the energy of love and compassion.

Life will never cease to be. It shall continue with new dawns of awakening, every moment of every life. It has no beginning and it has no end. From here to there is just a thought away. These thoughts combine to make the outside come to life. Life in the physical sense continues on a wavelength of pure ironian light. It pulsates to different tunes. The house of cards becomes the master. Teach this to the masses. They shall remember that they are just part of the whole process continuing into evermore. They chose their bodies, their experiences, their joys, their sorrows, their lives. They combine their essences into a fuller life to enjoy the lives of all others. This shall continue with new parameters being met, then discarded. Then all is to be made new. This newness is dependent upon all creation. One life upon the stars impacts one life on this planet earth. Know that all is filled with grace so new choices can be made.

Love the moment and each continuing moment shall be greater than the next. This is the greatness of eternity.

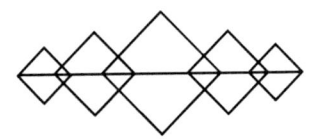

Q – *Who are the Pharaohs of Avalon?*

A – A group of people who lived in the fifteenth century in old Englande. Their role was to bring forth thoughts of oneness within the hierarchies who built Europe. They were also known as the Rasputins.

Q – *Explain "pure ironian light."*

A – Light that always is, does not waver.

Q – *Explain "the house of cards becomes the master."*

A – This statement denotes that civilizations are built upon certain belief systems. When those belief systems are shattered, then civilizations fall to be rebuilt.

August 18, 2003

Book of Divine Surrender

This book of "divine surrender" explains just what this means. The decree was written long ago that the time would come when all would be in alignment for the peoples to be in the position that they would surrender to the god within and follow the path of righteousness in their daily lives. They will see the same in every "individual" and know that each individual has their own agenda that is to be experienced only by that person. No one can take away another's experiences or right to experience. This book is being maintained in the archives of the Library of Congress of the United States. It is, indeed, an ancient book, one that was used in making the Declaration of Independence.

We hold these truths that all men are created equal. Man is and of the Creator. Each man has his own tasks separate from the next man. Each man is to follow his own instructions, as each man's instructions are not the same yet all men interrelate with one another. Each man, a sovereign being, shall integrate his experiences for his own soul growth and evolution. All is done for the good of the whole, the whole that is our Creator.

Paths, or experiences, are set for each soul before incarnation on the human level. The body type, male or female, is set into families that will nourish a soul's progression. This contract between the incoming soul and the souls of both the father and mother is made before entrance into the body that is being prepared within the womb of the mother. It makes no difference for the soul if the mother and the father are in a relationship outside of coupling. The circumstances have already been agreed upon.

With this understanding, all souls will evolve for their highest good. The internal god is the soul's connection to All That Is. Knowing that it is one's connection to the source is the true listening to the divine. Understanding that man is the divine incarnate will remove any interference that may be created by "outside" sources. "Thine own self be true" is knowing that divine creator resides in all man. Listen to the still voice. Listen and follow your own divine decree. Love thyself and know that all are God.

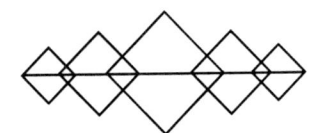

Q – This ancient book is being maintained in the archives of the Library of Congress of the United States. Where was this book found?

A – This book was found on tablets discovered in the ruins of a temple called "Jehovah's Words." This ancient temple was built by the Bruneins in the 5th dynasty of King Arthur. The world at that time was in turmoil because of the conflicts of the various sects and religions that were the fabric of the eastern world. King Arthur's role was to bring the differences into a more cohesive environment.

Brunei is a country that is located north of Malaysia on the shore of South China Sea.

Q – Is there anything else that needs to be said about this important book?

A – Yes. These writings became the fabric or foundation of your original laws of the United States of America. The founding fathers used them as guidelines.

August 24, 2003

Book of Divine Resurrection

Resurrection is a word that has many properties to it. In this instance, this book deals with the possibilities of the human mind. In the human's quest for further spiritual understanding, this book will answer those questions about your current body and the other bodies you possess. This book was written in the fourth century BC at the end of the cycle of Atum, the great solar king who was worshipped as the god of manifestation, the giver of life.

Greetings to the mind of Creators. This personage reveals the utmost in the process of soul communication. The triumphs of the soul reside in the mechanisms that are a part of each individual that encompasses each part of the soul. Each expression is a segment of the soul. On this Earth plane, one soul will have a multitude of expressions. These expressions cross many time lines or references.

The human stage of development lies within the progression of the soul in its attainment of form through the matrix of cross generation. The soul becomes the equalizer in its attempt to position its various incarnations to benefit its whole. When the whole of the soul reaches its pinnacle, it erupts into an overseer of a vast network of cross-over beings. It becomes the God-force. All god-forces form an internet of new creation. The forces are beyond the scope of density of matter. These energetic nodes are the force field that comprises all energy of all worlds. The human comprehension of this is within each self. Each person can tap into this knowledge of themselves, yet the concept will be elusive for most.

All matter is within the constructs of the soul. Because all life lives within matrix systems, then all life on the plane of matter appears to the individual soul consciousness as much the same – all life is biological form. The mysteries of all life, however, lie within each individualized soul. That knowledge can be tapped with the knowledge that is inherent within each physical body. Opening these centers is the responsibility of each soul.

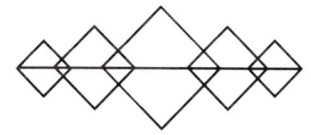

You are your maker. You are divine. You are one of many yet you are One. Be the instrument you have incarnated for, the life that brings you into contact with You. All knowingness shall return to you when your receptors are open. I AM Sananda, Light of the Most Radiant One. Blessings to you all in your acknowledgement of your own divineness. Blessings of Peace.

September 7, 2003

(18)

The Apex of Adam

During the turn of the century marked with a "K" lived a man who could transform the energy of a bucket of water into any liquid he could conjure in his mind. Many of the townspeople thought him as a trickster, but his trick was simple alchemy. He could perform these "miracles" with his mind. He was quite extraordinary, was well liked, but feared by many. This is his story.

The Story of the Bucket

It was in the beginning of my ninth year that I stumbled upon a container. I noted droplets of water held inside along with myriad insects, larvae, and rotting plant life. It struck me that this world within this container was a thriving life form full of new life lifting from the old that was being transformed. I watched with wonder the changes that were happening within this small world. I also wondered if my "larger" world was within a similar container but I could not see its sides. This incident led me on my path to understanding nature and life.

Throughout my formative years, I spent most of my time observing all of nature. I watched how it was affected by the stars, the moon, the sun. I noted that the positioning of the stars had a great effect on the temperature of the air and the amount of moisture within the air. We lived near a stream of cascading waters not far from a larger circle of water. The animals of the water seemed to have a patterning of their ways. At certain sun times and moon times, they would lie upon a rock and take within them the rays. They then would make their way to the shore line to lay their eggs. Three moon times later, the eggs would hatch and we would watch with glee as these tiny round shells would make their way into the waters. I found all of this very fascinating.

Upon observing the cycles of life, I contemplated my life and my interactions with other people as well as with nature. I could see I had an impact on my world, how I could change patterning with my thoughts. I would sit for long parts of the day thinking of something and then watching the small animals change their way of patterning. I knew that I had an effect on how they were seeing their world.

I then set about in finding the old container. I would practice with water and see how I could make waves with just my mind energy. I then added a small plant and with great focusing, I could see the roots of the plant grow down to the bottom of the container. Once the roots of the plant were established, I concentrated on the leaves and the flowers to break forth in their splendor. This all took place in part of one day.

Since I realized the power of my mind, I took a clean container of water and imagined my favorite fruit drink from the juice of the grapes. Suddenly the water turned into a red color, then a darker blue-red. My concentration had to remain steady or the liquid would return to water.

I started to demonstrate these mind powers on the townspeople. Most of them were fascinated, especially the children. Many of the older townspeople were afraid. They knew of my power and knew I had the knowledge to change the town and the surrounding forests. But I would not abuse the power I had within. I knew I could only use this power with love and devotion to the most-high creator. I also feel that all people have this gift of mind power but do not know how to use it.

I continue to amuse the people. I have even changed the water into wine for the horses. My friend was challenging me that I could not affect the waters of the sacred horses. So I stood over his horses' trough and changed the water into potent wine. His sacred horses went wild before their long sleep. My friend did not challenge me again.

I know the powers of the mind and I leave this book to be contemplated so that others will know of their powers. The source of these powers is within. I feel a grand connection to all life. I have the power yet feel a part of an even greater power. I am both the maker and the one being made. I now stare into the night skies and see life unending. I shall travel great distances into these stars to experience life in new ways. I feel as the grand Creator but know I am just a man. My name is Eurocles.

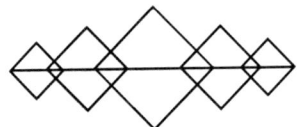

The name of this book "The Apex of Adam" is derived from the Book of Genesis. The Adam (pronounced "a dam'") is the seed from which the human is made. Apex is the height of the human experience and creatorship.

October 13, 2003

Book of the Holy Grail

In those parts of this Earth called The Grand Connection of the Andes lives a being named Anami. Anami is an Andean monarch who exists within the wilds of the rain forests. He reads life from his observations of the animals and the insects. There are people within his village who have migrated there not knowing they would stay for the remainder of their lives, yet they felt an inner yearning that moved them to this area. His lessons are as follows:

In the minds of man are the lives of all living things, all life everywhere within this grand Universe. We are the prawns, the creatures made to be the inhabitants of the many species. We acknowledge our role that we have agreed to take on. Our gratitude extends into this fine Earth of beauty and memory of life.

Ones shall make their pilgrimage to this land that so softly feels of the woman and the man intertwined in the bringers of life. Their role is to define the great One from which all exists. Within this compound can one extend themselves beyond this realm into the many other realms of life. We acknowledge the life beyond this plane, this sphere. We work within the guidelines of the Great One, the one of absolute balance, absolute love, and with no boundaries.

We now wish to extend ourselves out into the parts of this magnificent being, this Earth, into the knowledge of those others that inhabit this Earth. They shall see of our ways, our communications, our way of life. We invite the hearts of those individuals to make themselves known that a communication network can be set up. We look forward to our communications and the sharing of life.

Cum se, autish en mi cumbrance. I AM Anami.

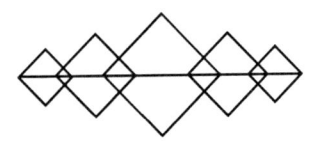

Per Anami, the meaning of the last sentence (a derivative of Latin) is:
With much love, I embrace all souls, all life.

The "Holy Grail" is life in the container of the soul. It is holy in that it is a part of God. The word Grail means container. Therefore man is god contained in a body.

March 13, 2004

Know Thyself

"Know thyself for it to be true." These words have been spoken through eons of time. Ponder the words. Find the true meanings behind your languages. Truths reside on all levels and one truth in one level may not be the same truth on another level. The language that presents itself as that which you read and write is based on the mechanics of another time and place. Perhaps this next book can give you a deeper perspective of this philosophy. We greet all who read this with open arms and hearts that they may grasp the contents of their own creations. This book can be found within the writings of Josephus, the scribe who lived on the ancient lands of Judea. Namaste.

Time marches like the soldiers in line. The uniqueness of time is score of evolution. Those who come to see and experience this great planet called Earth comb the forests that inhabit the lands and find an array of life that transcends species of evolvement. These species speak for the multitudes who come to serve as the wayshowers of new life.

Man brings with him a standard of life that shall prevail even when the winds blow so swiftly as to tear the ground asunder. Man speaks in the name of the father, the voice of all existence. The voice of the mother shall show herself as the voice of new creation within the ethers of All existence. Man shall cry out with the love that dwells within.

Man, do you not know that there are boundaries we must cross to continue our life spans? Do you not know the difficulties that exist to continue on this journey? Within all walks of life are bridges we must face to continue on in God's kingdom. We are here to raise the existence of mankind so that he will know his roots. Man will falter in his quest yet I say unto you that should you not quest, there will be no future. Hunger for the divine to be known. Hunger and thirst for the knowledge of divinity. Know you are that divinity yet you must remain in this body of man. Do not quiz yourself that the road you are on is the wrong road. There are no wrong roads. We may interpret them that way, yet we would not know of our significance if we did not take the many roads we make available.

Choose what you think is the most significant for you. If you think that, then so it is. The recorders of old have left their knowledge that all knowing is in the moment. Many seek their divinity only to find that it cannot be apart from themselves. Foolish ones will remain in the shadows until they are ready to grasp the magnificence of their being.

The parts of the whole are each and every one of us. It is ALL. See your reflection in the trees, in the grasses, in the reflection in the pond. Warm your toes in the sweet mud of this Earth. She grows the foods, our own bodies with her substance. Honor ALL. Existence is your ability, your truth in making the world what it is, and what it shall be. Love the moment and see that it is life, it is love. Creators, know you are absolute. Know you are the makings of your own creations. See others as yourself and you will comprehend all life in absolute awe. Release all judgments, for you only judge yourself. Know you are an eternal seed blossoming into new creations. You are divine. You can be no less.

June 19, 2004

Book of Titles

In every culture, there are ones who are called by the work that they perform, i.e. have titles. In the very earliest kingdoms on earth, this concept was used. Identification of ones who have specific job functions or are part of nobility have found the system befitting. This practice shall continue as part of the upcoming changes in the physical world. However, they will be used in an altogether different way. Mankind shall find that their current life is just one aspect of their total life. Their many lives shall show that all have been called many titles in their life streams. What importance they have for you shall be discussed in this next book. Namaste.

Across the miles of seas, in the wildernesses are the seeds to becoming the man of the ages. Each one of man shall come to recognize that it is he who is the provider, the conqueror, the speech writer, the concubine, the wisdom of all of the ages. He shall recognize that it is he who is the mover and the shaker, the one who shall seek his own salvation. He is his own savior and shall remain so as he traverses all of the cosmos.

Man shall know that it is he who is the God of salvation as there can be no other gods before Me. Equality is in the womb of creation. What one creates becomes his task. A task is the experience of one's own creation. What one devises for a lifetime shall be the name he gives himself. He is his own task force, the living force that permeates all creation.

In the times that shall become the book of the ages, man will see of himself the perfect nugget of gold. Perfection starts in the heart and extends out into the full body. The resonance shall be the perfect sound, the perfect vibration. The chorus is the combination of all the sounds, of all the tasks, of all the lifetimes. It reaches into the abyss and into the high heavens. Where else can one become all? The astounding fact of all life is in the living of the various aspects of one's own journey. How can one truly become the infinite creator? By tapping into the wonderful worlds of Creator.

Magnificent star beings of the many universes, come and enjoy your fruits. Live the lives you have dreamed. Be the Gods, the creative forces that have joined together in this moment of creation. Arrange your lives into sequences of love realized. You shall become the leaders of an enormous experiment. This experiment involves the gentle life forces as well as the thunderous ones of the fifth level of consciousness. Come together and make of yourselves in the new world. Forces that once were forbidden now come to the surface. Face yourselves. Realize what you are and where you are going. Become the gods of tomorrow.

Once this experiment has been fully established, then recede in your consciousness. Know you will have accomplished the uplifting of all creation. We of the arcs of creation will be with you on all of your travels in each of your lives. Blessed is each aspect of you in the fulfillment of the grand plan. In loving divine service, we now call out that this will be put into place. So Be It.

June 10, 2002

㉒

Book of the Azores

Sananda and I are on a mountaintop, partially snow-capped. These mountains are located on the eastern side of Iceland. The rock is reddish-brown in color, probably a limestone. There is a town to the west and the ocean to the east. This mountain range is positioned north to south, then angles to the west at the southern tip.

The sun rises on the western ridge. We watch the boiling sea as the turmoil recedes into the consciousness of the past. Behold, we await a new future, a future that holds promise of a new day and time of total release of the darkness of mankind. We mandate with these writings that humankind will rise to a being again capable of mastering their bodies and surroundings with a degree of perfection associated with their origins.

Rise mankind. We will not return to the state of consciousness where there is no respect for our sense of being. *(I sense anger and sadness with the sinking and demolition of Atlantis.)* Mankind, from this moment on, must cease from its destruction. We shall move into a world of understanding self. Oh Gods of Abraham, who doest this moment in time? Bring the love of the Father and the gentleness of the Mother to blend together those aspects of being into a complete being of compassionate understanding. Those of us who have incarnated upon this jewel, where did the programs fail? Let no man or woman again feel the insidious disruptions of life.

Man, alone, must face the consequences of his actions. Where does he begin? The hour has come, indeed, to turn the tide of destruction. We ask the gods of Abraham to help us in the formation of a new set of codes for mankind. We shall not falter for our role here on this sphere is a role that must be completed to fulfill the experience of density of the gods. Bring to us, our star brothers and sisters, the codes of light that shall open the seeds of deliverance. Bring us the food that shall take us to a level of understanding so as not to interfere with our physical bodies. We shall climb into the known from the unknown. We shall inherit our rightful place in the sea of life. We shall think with our minds intertwined with our hearts so that mankind and their souls can feel the love of creation. Creation must be refined to a level of consciousness that blends emotion into the physical. We shall be as angels in the love of God. We shall inherit the sons of man and the sons of God to bring a balance of maturation in the thought forms of love. The love in the heart of God shall be made manifest in all life. No more shall creation be entangled in a web of disguise and deceit.

I call upon the heavens to bring this balance to manifest in the hearts and minds of all beings that are to reside on earth. The Masters of Wisdom shall take their positions to bring this about. Our place in this universe of universes shall be the alchemist of life in the dimensions of mankind in the flesh. This call shall and is our mandate for a new earth, a new spirit of being in the great cosmos of love existing in the formation of creationism of the refinement of life.

In the name of the One, our great Creator of the Universes, we are the brothers and sisters that now take the vow that this earth shall become the shining star of Jerusalem.

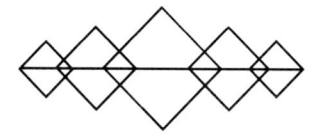

Upon receiving this book, I saw a vision of silver necklace on a woman's chest. It looked similar to the following drawing:

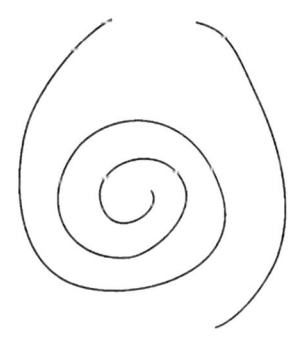

Q - I asked Sananda about Abraham, because Abraham (the man) supposedly lived after these tablets were written.

A - Abraham was and is indeed a being that lives on this Earth plane when he is needed. He is one of the Elohim that has an intense interest in the people that reside on this planet. His job is to still the chaos so that all who incarnate on Earth can use their creative abilities – the reason Earth became into being.

March 27, 2002

Book of Tibet

Sananda stands near a small boulder on a hillside near a Tibetan Monastery. I "see" a stone head of an ancient Buddha in the distance.

At the turn of the twenty-first century shall it become to be known that the energy make-up of the cellular structure in all life shall change. These changes represent the new biology. This biology is part of what is called "Plan 2" set forth by the Great Creator and the Lords of Wisdom from the many galaxies throughout the twelve solar systems of the metamorphoses of the seven physical dimensions.

The time will come when the planets in this particular solar system will combine with those of the star gate system called Sirius. Through these gates shall rise the protein "anphybium," a substance that is found in the DNA (deoxyribonucleic acid) of every living cell that lives within the seven dimensions. This protein shall activate the chromosomes in the latent strands of DNA/RNA (ribonucleic acid). Upon activation, shall rise the kundalini experience where the body's energy (flow of electro-magnetic) impulses flow down from the stem of the spinal column throughout the nervous system. The body will feel "light." A shudder will take place and the cells will be full of liquid light. The skin will take on a color of bluish-white to red and will radiate an iridescent glow. Initially the experience may be frightening to many but that feeling will soon diminish into a complete knowingness. The earth shall be transformed in that moment. The very ground of Mother Earth shall also shudder. The light, which Lady Gaia has held within, shall burst forth and encompass the entire planet, including her atmospheres.

(This is what is meant by: "Arise from the dead," which is written in your Bible. All of mankind shall rise from their sleep or death and understand the truth of their beingness.)

When that time comes, this period shall be known as "the voice that doesn't speak." All shall communicate through their minds. Life shall move beyond the survival stage into an age of science of the divine. Through the tears shall man see their most radiant forms. From these writings shall those that understand be ready for this great transformation.

It is so.

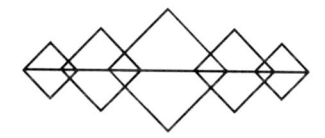

Q – What is Plan 1?

A – Plan 1 was administered to be the recycling of souls. By this, we mean that all souls who incarnated on this earth plane would shortly return to their home planets. But during the processes of inhabiting this Earth, many got caught up in their egos. Thus, the structure of a "shell" was put around this planet for protection of the cosmos from some of the miss-creations of the ego-centered beings on this planet. Therefore Plan 2 was put into place by Creator and many souls who were not mastered by their own egos.

Q – It is written "galaxies throughout the twelve solar systems." Please explain.

A – There are twelve solar planes of existence, each comprising twelve galaxies of which your earth is a part of what you call the Milky Way galaxy.

There are millions upon millions of stars and planets in this expanding universe.

Q – *The last paragraph of this book says "through the tears shall man see their most radiant forms."*

A – Tears will be shed in joy and amazement of what each man and woman will see/acknowledge when the veil of forgetfulness is gone. Man will see all of his (her) forms, all lives. Man will indeed understand just how wondrous he is!

April 25, 2004

The Forces of Evil

Mankind in his search to understand the truth has dwelled in the trenches of self-sacrifice for the benefit of all. This self-sacrifice was felt as a duty, a warrior in the preservation of God. There is no need to preserve God, for God is the All, dark and light and light and dark. It exists as thought. With the benefit of the new light being felt on this planet, mankind will understand the divine plan. As it unfolds, man will see that life is indeed a force that lives in each one person. It is not bad and it is not good. It just is. However, ones of the light are bringing in their love to bring about the change of consciousness in each and every person who allows to hold such magnitude. Man's thoughts and prayers are being answered. The forces that wish to keep mankind locked in a hypnotic state have their "powers" in place. In truth, their powers shall also change as the love vibration increases on this planet.

In as many ways to conceal danger, man has continued on living his life. He has worked through troubles and tribulations. He has seen the fall of many empires that were too radical for the peoples. He has seen the demise of trusted friends and officials. Contemplation of the why of this has troubled man for eons. What is happening is on many levels. It encompasses many generations of the human species as well as the less seen species that thrives on the inner depths of earth and in the ethers of the surrounding area. To quench the thirst of peace, many lightworkers have made their presence known in all places of this planet. People listen to their word but the true understanding is too deep for the people to grasp.

Therefore many times have the light people incarnated on this planet only to find that the majority of human-kind were not ready for the light to be totally understood and experienced. Man has found ways to stop the peace so the infiltrators could bring in their wares that would wow the senses. The emotions of man were made through the development of the five senses. Pleasure took on a new form that did not come from the heart. Man in his earnest continued on in the development of the sensory glands. He felt it was his right to steal and pillage for the benefit of the few. Life became a struggle and the consequences were gratifying as man maintained his attachment to this planet and the maneuvering of its peoples.

The light was maintained on the planet that would significantly raise the lifeblood of the Earth mother. She has continued to grow despite the rummaging and the pillaging of her skin. She has remained steadfast in her current to the divine plan. Her decision was made at the time of her inception that she would emerge as a grand spark in the universe of divine love incarnate.

There are ones who saw of her plan and wanted to be a part of it. They watched as she began her physical changes. These ones were in awe of what they saw happening. They wanted this life for themselves. These ones knew they had to become as the travelers in distress in order for the Earth to allow them to be a part of her body. When Earth saw that her body was being used and her life force being abused, she changed her form so these ones could not live upon her surface. As she shook, she attracted those who would assist her in her transition. Many decided to stay. They felt her wonderful love and the beauty she held. More and more beings felt her love and in that love she invited the benevolent ones to be a part of her, to assist her in her ascension.

Radical changes became too intense for many of the planet dwellers *(ones who stayed with the planet)*. On hearing their cry, many beings came and brought with them their technologies that would tame the changes going on. They brought their power to calm a storm. Their technologies were so great that even the lighted ones were fooled by what they witnessed. Even those who came to support the men and women who were to be the soothsayers were fooled by these technologies. Finally the lighted ones could see of the destruction that was going on but could not change the flow of the information that was being utilized.

The technologies in themselves served mankind in that they gave man a new direction, a new freedom. The freedom was with other creations, other planets. They were introduced to many ways of living, of reproduction, of transcendence of the body. They witnessed incredible transformations of the body. Technology became an instrument of new life yet the new life did not maintain its structure. Deterioration was common and the new technologies could not reverse them. Yet within man's being was the drive to understand their makeup. There was more to them than the new technologies. Many became disillusioned with the new art sciences. There were wonderful inventions with new understandings of the workings of the universe yet they felt there was more to their lives than what was being pursued by the scientists. The internal "instincts" said more would be exposed.

Many off-worlders came and infiltrated all life on this planet. The internal earth mother allowed the use of her body to be the school house of new life. Within her central being, she felt compassion for all life who would partner with her. She knew that life could be so complete and loving, that no technology would change that aspect. So she set up a base rotation of her axis to increase the magnetics of her structure. This would hold off any experiments that weren't for the highest good of herself and those who now resided upon and in her surface. Man became dense to the point of not knowing of the abuse that they all used and were a part of. The ones who came here for the use of Earth's body for scientific advancement that was not for the greater good were forced to leave. They left their mark in the stone structures that could withstand what was known as time.

The word "evil" is nothing more than not understanding the true Life Force. Through the scientific experiments, knowledge was gained of how the universe is to expand. Only through light can the darkness be quelled. Through all of the transformations of the technologies, the Life Force has become greater. This is what is called the "allowance program." The Life Force is a constant yet new thoughts or manifestations occur with the input of all life however benevolent or non-benevolent they are. Progression in the light will become new worlds, new life. All sparks of the divine continue out to experience or just witness the Life Force as it moves into new ways of being. This is called infinity as man weaves himself into the fabric of the golden thread. This great and magnificent planet Earth shall turn on its side and start again. A balance shall return to her as those lighted beings come to assist her in the blossoming of the divine plan. Together shall planet Earth and her inhabitants grow in the finer life patterns. Evil shall be brought into balance with the magnificent light that shall be this planet. The soul of Earth, Gaia, has made the clarion call in which a conglomeration of life has responded. Those who want to keep the Earth in her darkness shall find that they will have to absorb the balance of light or they will have to leave. The mandate was made by the Light of the Federation of All

Nations. In the century known as "Light" will Gaia make her full transition. She will stand in a new place which will enable her to maintain the frequencies for her to grow her light until she becomes like a diamond that has been faceted and polished. No allowance of abuse will remain within and on her. All life within her spectrum shall be on the same frequencies. The Life Force of Love shall bring only fully lighted beings to incarnate with her. Any mysteries of being will have been revealed. Creation will take another step to understanding its Force.

We of The Federation of Light within The Galactic Federation shall be of service during the great transformation. We offer only love to bring this transformation about. Peace be you who shall read of these words. Nothing can stand in your way to become the peace bearers of Divine Love.

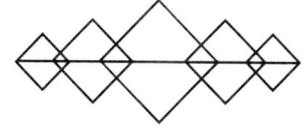

Man in his quest to become the light bearers shall know that it is He who is God, the Life Force. There shall be no other God before you. Transformation will come upon this plane with the release of all hatred brought on by fear. When man fears no more and takes control of his own life while respecting the lives of all other men and animals, then he will gently guide himself into the new realms while maintaining his presence on this great Earth plane.

Peace of mankind is about this release of all hatred, greed, fear, abuse, anger, loathing, and all of those experiences you all have gone through to understand that there is only love. The love of God is truly loving yourself. I brought this concept to this Earth plane in my existence as Jeshua ben Joseph, the one known as Jesus. I stand by this knowledge that there can be no other Gods before thee. Thee is you.

September 18, 2002

Book of Entrapment

Sananda led me into a place that looks to be an underground cavern. As I was being led, I could not see anything around me until we were in the cavern. The walls of the cavern are earthen (brownish) but the outer layer looks like glass. The dimly lit area reflects like glass but the surface is bumpy but with no jagged edges. The walls are rounded, dome-like. I ask Sananda, "Where are we?"

Sananda answers, **"We are in the most southern region of the area you know as Cydonia. Indeed we are "underground" or under the outer surface of the planet Mars. It is here that man transfigured into the Homo sapiens that we know today. The last vestiges[1] of the time warp are centered here in this region. The outer area or surface reflects the once magnificent civilizations that have existed in this solar system. Because of the rebellion of those beings who changed their genetic structures to fit the pool of Galeceans, the seeds were tainted or transformed into a species that no longer could survive on the surface. The survivors went into the belly of the planet to continue their race. This book is about this great civilization and what created their downfall."**

The stars of Bethlehem shine brightly in the skies of the Infinite

---

1 Vestige – *The Living Webster Encyclopedic Dictionary of the English Language:* A mark, trace, or visible evidence of something which is no longer present or in existence.

Spirit. The once mighty fortress of this part of the universe stands guard in the vortex of the most holy high. Here is the story of Babylon, that great center on earth whose tale of woe has come to this area of our planet. Oh magnificent One, let us not forsake your wisdom, your kingdom, your land of lands. Let us rise in the name of the holy one of the ages. We shall turn back the pages of time into the known love of the species of Abraham. Into this portal shall rise the likeness of the Elohim made manifest into the face of the angels. Let this be a sign of the return of the age where there is no strife, no fear, only love of the One. Into this era shall we bless form with the soul wrapped in flesh of the body. The flesh shall be of light.

We have come this far into the outer reaches of the universe to try our hand at creatorship. We call upon the Lords of Light to assist us in this making. Why does our request go unanswered? Why have we been forsaken? What has happened? Are we blind that we cannot see? The ability to create has been bestowed upon us. Believe it and it shall be. We have been told of this ability but we have yet to utilize it as it was designed to be.

We build great edifices to the magnificent. We build wonders onto the stars. We bring about force of the grids to power our edifices. Shall we count the many before the few? What is at stake? Our brothers and sisters lie down their bodies in praise of the holy One. Answer us O Lord. Shall we mate the flesh?

To this we have answered our own questions. We shall make the flesh into form of the most high. We shall praise the forms in their development. We shall break a covenant that was given us long ago by the ones of the western skies. Their light shines upon us with the magnitude of the magnetic bands of the fire of the sun. The covenant of ancients who saw that this planet was to be a ground of manifestations into the physical dimensions of form and matter is now and ever shall be a solicitation of time waves woven into our spectrum of our dimensional expertise. Know that this will be done.

Great one of spirit, let us draw near to the precipice of the Almighty. Let the bells ring loudly with the sound of the coming of the masters of Orion. Our voices call out to rise in the mist, to give birth to the innocents. Let us breathe in the essence of freedom.

Let us hang our heads low to receive the blessings of Abraham, the one who we have called forth. His image shall be as a beacon to the masters. They shall appear in our heavens, our skies. We hold great visions that our life on this planet will once again live with the many species to sustain our bodies as well as create a world that supports all life in the physical. We come forth to acknowledge the legions of beings that have been as our leaders into the known world of sensor perception. Our bodies cry out in the face of change. We are moving to another phase. We are to gather our strength and march forward in the receiving of the coming of the red dragon.

The night shall be the way of Morgan, the one who brings the veil to cover the eyes of the innocent. Receive him not, (for) inside the light grows. The intensity shall be great. Open thine eyes and let the light in. You shall see the light return to this beautiful planet. We shall move to our rightful place among the living planets of Airophim. The lines of the passages (communications) are open. He who so chooses can access these great connectors to fulfill their own desires. In the light shall all Be.

Let the forces of light come through and permeate all that has been left in darkness. Let us once again take our role in this galaxy as the ones of magic. We shall once again assume our positions to manifest our mathematics and geometry into the life forms of crystallized light. Our forces shall be felt again in the light of the Radiant One.

Adam out.

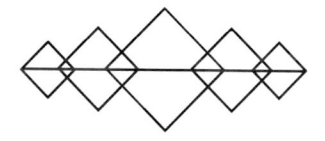

I feel that this book was left in the crystals left in the cavern. The crystals exude a pale light that can be seen by the naked eye.

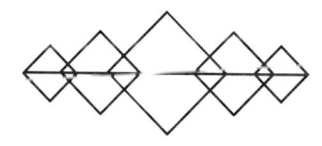

Q – *Sananda, you mentioned that the outer area or surface of Cydonia on the planet Mars reflects a once magnificent civilization. Would you expand on this?*

A – **People whom you know as the great Ones or Elohim came to this place and set up a scientific base centered around the loving force of God. They built the pyramidal structures you have seen in your photographs of this area. They worked within these structures because they knew these structures could hold the higher vibrations of light energy. They utilized their ability to make of themselves into the different life forms of a biological nature. They were able to reproduce what you would term quantum light. They understood the properties of this light.**

Q – *Then what do you mean by the rebellion of those beings…?*

A – **Those beings I refer to are the grand marchers, or ones who went to Mars to infiltrate the lighter ones or Elohim.**

Q – The book mentions the story of Babylon. Did the people of Babylon go to this area of Mars?

A – No, only their "tale of woe" or demise on the earth was known to these beings and they did not want the same thing happen to them. Ground movements buried the city of Babylon.

Q – This book is a little difficult to understand. Why is this book included and what does it really mean to us in this time?

A – This book tells of your beginnings of becoming human in biological form that you are today. Just know there are many, many biological forms that have the capacity to think and create as you do.

October 28, 2002

Book of the Covenant

The light of the ages past and present can be seen in all things made manifest by the richness of the word of the Creative force that resides in all. Our stations on the battlefield of despair shall bring forth the new word that all shall be made new, not to return to the old patterns of the wretched ones. Life shall be born again to the splendors of the living God in all of life, not to be taken lightly but to savor and enjoy the love of all. He who imagines with the highest of intents will know with confidence that which he is and must do. The time of the storm has now come.

We watch with a close eye the past that shall never again be repeated. We know from which we came. We stand by ready to take aim at the unconscious. From now to evermore shall the reins of love be the only way to the blinding light of infinite wisdom. Make manifest the incarnations of the Beloveds. They shall be as the leaders, the wayshowers of this infinite wisdom. They shall lead by the example of their lives.

Make perfect these ones so they know their origins. They shall be as the elixir of magic to those who cannot see. They shall be known as the Fire Stones, intense yet rigid in their ability to show truth. Oh wise men of old, bear witness unto this divine lineage. Work with their other selves to keep them in the light of lights. They shall emerge into all cycles that will be a part of the Kingdom. We send blessings unto the land, the sacred soil of our dear Mother.

Our hearts intertwine with the Radiant Light. Our day has come, indeed, into this Holy Land. Our countenance shall remain in this place and bleed through all dimensions. Our names shall be the sacred sounds of Creator. Sing the tones of the great life. Breathe in then out the fields of the Dynamo. We are and always shall be One World, One Love, One Life. From this One, there are Many. It does not matter how we will circle around. Through these many lives will we regain our Oneness.

Absolute truth has been spoken. Our vibrations enter into all creation. We are the ones by these names we give ourselves: Dan-i-el, Gab-ri-el, Eze-ki-el, Ar-i-el, Ur-i-el, Mich-i-el, Raph-a-el. Feel our vibrations with these words we project. We are One for Evermore.

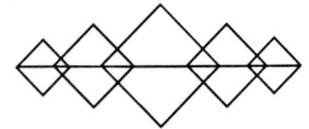

Our beloved archangels have left their energy vibrations with this Earth. Their love will always be felt on our beloved Gaia. Their words speak only of Love and shall not be translated to mean anything else. These words can be found in the great archives of the living library, the Akashic Records.

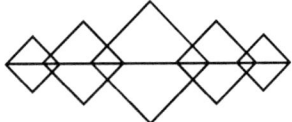

Q – What are the "fields of the dynamo"?

A – The fields of eternal truth, the forces of God.

Q - Does the statement: "It does not matter how we will circle around" talk about time?

A – Indeed time is circular and it does not matter the number of incarnations of a soul.

March 9, 2003

(27)

Book of the Road to Beth-le-hem

As I wander through the desert of Northern Africa, I come upon a rock. Inscribed is a story about the people who have lived two millennia ago in this great part of the Earth. At that time, this area was a thriving metropolis that had irrigation to farm the green pastures, a stable economy, and a government that ruled for the people. It was much like a grand utopia that many yearn for today. Here is their story.

Life in its infinite glory calls upon all men and women to be the grandest that they can be. We expect that all peoples who come to this great land know that they are most welcome. They shall find true happiness in their work, in their home, and in their lives. That will be so in that all life here shall follow in the divine aspects of our Creator.

The release of all conflicts is necessary and is accomplished by the walking and living in the basic laws of the universe. "He that stows upon this jewel shall become part of the jewel. He that does harm shall forfeit their right and move to a location that can better serve them. But if it in is their hearts, we shall teach the wisdom and understanding that Creator is their guiding force."

The laws of the Universe are:
1. I am the Lord thy God. There can be no other.
2. Your physical lives shall be in concordance to my will for you are Me.
3. From this moment, all life on this planet shall follow in the teachings of the great Shambhala, through the words and actions of the Great Masters.
4. Listen to these Masters, for you tune into yourselves.
5. Yourselves contain all.
6. You are the creators, create in love.
7. Your friend also is a creator. Respect each one's creations.
8. Each has your own path. Follow your own, not another's.
9. Love yourself, love the planet, and love the universe. The universe sings your song.
10. You are the makers of heaven and earth. Choose wisely that which will be for the greater good of the whole.
11. I Am that I AM, and So It Is.

Respect, intuition, and joy are our focus. Our creations shall pass the test of time. Time was created for us to know that what we endeavor shall manifest itself upon this plane of existence. The length of the physical life depends upon your need in this existence. Some needs are met with very short life spans. Others are met with life spans that shall transit many returns of the constellations. Your needs are your own, for your own evolvement of your very soul. Respect all souls.

The grander life can be felt and seen with your return to the higher realms of existence. You will know when all is done in the name of our great Creator God, YHWH. Eternity is life expanding into new ways of being.

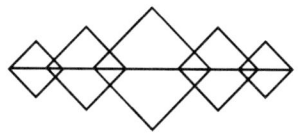

This original book was written in Arabic. The book also contains the seven laws of reverse logic. The continuation of the book shall be given at another time of understanding. Understand now (this present day) the dramas that are playing themselves out. These dramas will soon be out of existence, for they have played too long and have become part of the human's psyche. This part of consciousness is being cleansed and shall not return. The wonders of this world shall continue.

The name Beth-Le-Hem refers to the House of the Lord.

October 10, 2002

(28)

Book of the Turban

I requested that this book be included because of the confusion that this style of dress implies. This book was written forty thousand years ago along the banks of the river Nile. This area was once a thriving community of devoted people who worshipped the planet (Earth) as well as lived by the positioning of the stars. Their community was one of agriculture and fine ceramics, of which they were quite proud. They bathed in the waters of the Nile which at that time flowed into the Adriatic Sea. Geography at that time was much different than it is today. Because of the many great earth movements, this civilization has been buried since their demise approximately ten thousand years ago during the after effects of what you term The Great Flood. Should the land become volatile once again, which it could, then fragments of this civilization will come to surface. Their story, which has been left behind, shall awaken those who communicated and worked with these beings in past incarnations. Their story is one of peace and prosperity. They had great love for one another and their community.

We have knowledge that the earth is changing and that our lives may be in danger. We leave this book to be discovered once the waters recede. This book details our lives, our community, and love of this earth and the stars.

Our city is set up in blocks. Each block represents our duties that we all contribute for the whole of the community. When we are young, we are introduced to each block. We work within each block for at least one year. After we have worked in all the blocks, of which there are twenty, then we work with our elders who prepare us for our greater works in the block of our choice. This way, we understand and appreciate what each block has to offer the community yet we choose where we feel we can be the most productive. Our lives are fulfilled with pursuing our love. If, after an extended period, we want to move to another block, we go before the elders and request that we be retrained in another pursuit. The elders discuss our requests, and if they feel the request is for your highest good and the highest good of the community, then permission is granted. You then become an apprentice of your choice before you are fully allowed to enter into the block on your own. Many ones, both women and men, change blocks as many as ten times in their life spans.

These twenty blocks include:
1. Masonry
2. Ceramics
3. Child care
4. Healthcare/body balancing
5. Science – study of mathematics and physics
6. Agriculture
7. Animal husbandry
8. Food preparation
9. Community storytelling (performing arts)
10. Block building/carving
11. Astrology/astronomy
12. Cloth making
13. Jewelry design and making for ceremony
14. Tool making (from rock and metals)

15. Techniques and building of water movement for agriculture and animals
16. Dye making
17. Sports
18. Energy (electrical) distribution
19. Oratory
20. Reproduction assistance

Our dress reflects which block in which we work. Typical attire is long sheaths for both men and women. Because of the heat of this land, we wear headdresses to protect us from the sun and the sifting sands that stretch before the Nile.

Our land is robust with foliage of many varieties. We grow our foods in the outer lands. Water is provided for by the use of canals as well as ample rainfall. Many gardens are placed throughout our living and working homes. These gardens are frequented by all for meditation and self-reflection. We go to the gardens to think and connect with the Elders of the other races who assist us on these lands. These Elders do not live with us but communicate with us. We call them the nomads of the sky because we can only see them in our meditations.

We hold many celebrations throughout the year. We come together at the equinoxes and the solstices. We work with the elementals for thanks and renewal of the lands. We thank the water spirits for their contributions. We thank the sky spirits for the rain and cloud formations. They tell us much in the clouds. We can even hear their voices. This helps us prepare for the heavy rains that we need to soak the ground in our growing seasons.

We have become masters at repairing the body. With the use of sound, any accident that breaks the flesh is repaired almost instantly with vibrations from the flout.

We were told by the Elders that our time here on this beautiful Earth is to come to an end. We know this Mother needs to break open to let her waters flow freely over her skin. We have been blessed to partake of her gifts. We leave these books to be found after she has been renewed. We are told we will go to another place and live out our lives. We look forward with much anticipation to our new way of living. Onto the gods of the great Sun we cast our faces to the west for the bringers of the new day.

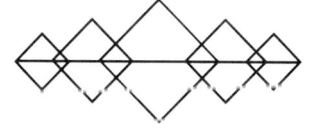

From this text do we know that ones before us have lived communal and joyful lives. Their life spans were a few hundred years. They lived in total harmony. If one lives in total reverence with all and their surroundings, then the joy of life cannot be surpassed. The wonders of existence await all who live in their hearts. May the peace of these peoples be felt in all who read their words. Namaste.

November 10, 2002

Book of the Dream

In the time of Atlantis, there was a warrior named Antibus. He was a wonderful carpenter who created magic from his tools of unmatched technology. He could manifest a great light within his being and transfer it into the crystals that could cut and shape all types of materials. His story follows.

My name is Antibus and I leave my technology of spirit within these writings to be found, interpreted, and used in the formation of materials found in and on this great body of rock, mineral, and water. I find that all life comes from our living hands, shaped by our living hearts and minds. Who shall find that meaning inside of them shall also find the Creator of all. I work in my own refuge along with my beautiful family. We support one another in all of our endeavors. Each of us has our own unique gift and we share in that knowledge. How wonderful that is!

My gift is in the art of making matter into something that is not only beautiful to look at but quite useful as well. I am known as the wise one who is crazy. I like that definition as it serves me well. The townspeople come to visit quite often, anticipating what I may create next. I chuckle in my own heart of their anticipation because I always surprise them with what they do not expect. That is why they call me crazy.

I now create this writing. I have told others what I plan to do with this writing and they say, "How can that be?" "How will man in the future be able to interpret your madness?" I know that my madness is infectious so I know that man in the future will be able to understand.

The art of material making is a bridge between this world and all others. To access the other dimensions is to engage in a steady state of amorphism. From the catalyst of the mind set in the various components of the dimensional waves, the ability to move the particles can be attained. The transfiguration then occurs with the use of the mind power controlling the desired result. All exists within the possibility. This world is so much more than what meets the eye. My senses can clearly see the result before it is manifest. My work can be found inside of all who endeavor in the arts. It is within where all power lies. The art of particle exchange is quite unique in that all particles change their molecular structure to meet the level of velocity of the earth in its orbit around the sun. The bright rays of the nuclear fusion that exists in the solar frequencies are accessed for their ability to connect the molecular strings of matter on this plane.

What enables me to do this is the power (or seeming there of) to slow down the frequencies of the matter to break the process of regeneration. I remold the particles, enhance them with the energy of the crystal bodies into shapes (and sounds) of another form. I play with my designs. Is work not play? My magic will seem outrageous to the scientists in the labs, but it really is quite easy. They ask for my technology but I cannot give it to them when they are not of the higher vibration of divine wisdom. I have seen into the next world where this technology will be commonplace. Then all of mankind will be crazy!

I am Antibus, the magic man of craziness!

December 23, 2002

Book of the Renaissance

During the ages when the French over took the European nations, a man named Francois DeBuois founded an organization called "The Knights of Splendor," a secret organization which has left its mark on humanity. This organization understood the laws of the universe but was reluctant to share all they knew. Some of their knowledge infiltrated the Knights of Templar that still exists today.

Man, in his ability to understand the universe, has taken on a journey to know his roots and the expectations he has given himself in the fulfillment of the rites of morrow. He has gained in the magnificence of this material world yet has lost his ability to know of his divine rights. We shall bring to the forefront these divine rights and live by them.

1. By thy own self be true.
2. The turn of the ages shall be the responsibility of each individual.
3. The flight of the humming bird shall present to mankind his prowess with discovery.
4. Turn the action into manifestation for the good of all men.
5. Thy actions speak louder than words.
6. The force of all nature lies within each one of us.

7. Bring forth the wisdom so all man can partake.
8. Cease the action of jealousy. It brings harm to all.
9. Find what makes you happy and follow that dream.
10. Mankind in his search for the magnificent shall find it in the mundane lives of themselves.
11. Reach out to your brothers.
12. Find true happiness in the small things you accomplish.
13. The atom is the smallest particle that man will be able to see. Know that the atom can be divided many times.
14. Who shall speak the truth shall be free from all expectations.
15. From these statements, man shall find that he continues to live.
16. Life beyond life is.
17. All is and as it should be.
18. Take heed in the advice of the beloved, you.
19. Know that all exists by the vision you hold.
20. Peace in its simplest form is love.
21. Love yourself and all of mankind for they are your brothers and sisters.
22. Love Mother Earth for she gives her body for you.
23. Here is the now, live it to its fullest.
24. Honor all nature. All is alive.
25. Honor that which gave you life.
26. The truth of living is in the living.
27. Just be for that is the only thing you are.
28. Trust that there is more to this life that you live, there is the Creator.
29. Man has infinite wisdom, use more than you think you have.
30. Love is the deepest of all emotion, use it in all you do.
31. Walk your vision and it shall come to you.
32. Work and play should be synonymous.

33. The force of all life resides in all places.
34. The eye is only a window. Doors will open when you are ready to move on.
35. All intellect is available to all.
36. Know that you are a part of all that is.
37. There is much more to life then mankind can comprehend.
38. Live your lives fully.
39. The message to live fully can be answered by prayer.
40. Communicate with thyself.
41. No one is more powerful than you.
42. Retreat within for the answers.
43. The night shall cease and the day shall expand.
44. True education lies in your ability to hear God.
45. To hear means to heed.
46. Love is truly divine.
47. Judgment was brought upon by man. To judge is to erase your accomplishments.
48. True accomplishments are in line with divine creation.
49. To create is what we are here to do.
50. Create wisely and you shall know God.

This treatise shall be signed within your heart.
Amen
Amen
Amen
And Amen

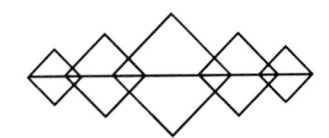

Q – Is there any comment on this book?
A – During the end times of the old creation, that which you know as The Crusades was to destroy these teachings all in

the name of the church. It is now time to let these controls of the old churches be known. Nothing is to be hidden from the masses of humankind. They are ready to know who they are and from where they came. Now these truths are revealed. They are everlasting, absolute truths. Nothing shall stand in the way of these truths being exposed for they are the word of God, begotten of all humankind. All secret organizations, open your archives. There is absolutely nothing to hide. It is time for the people to take their own power and utilize it for themselves, their God within.

Know these truths and understand them. They are your commandments. Man cannot live by bread alone. Man can and will live by love, only love.

Your countries will drastically change and all will follow these principles. By living within these guidelines, there will be no more wars, no more prejudices, no more animosity among neighbors. Incredible communities will arise that will be filled with love, sharing, and a greater understanding of the divine. Commit in your hearts that you will be filled with this love and understanding and it shall be so!

Q – You say these truths "are the word of God, begotten of all humankind." Isn't humankind begotten of God?

A – Humankind are the founders of this new way and this new way is God clothed in flesh. Understand your power that is yours and yours alone. You each are unique individuals that are this awesome power, and this awesome power can only be used in love.

I AM THE WHOLE, made up of uniquely made individuals. So it is and ever shall BE.

December 29, 2003

Book of Innocence

It was the time before the onslaught of Monrovian Beings that this book was written. In your linear time, this took place approximately two million years ago on the island of Paiz which is located in the Indian Ocean. This civilization made great strides into their manifestation of their physical being in concordance to their emotional bodies. In their internal quest, they stood as a threat to the race who used slaves for their physical work. Thus, the Monrovian Beings were slaughtered to keep the new mankind in control.

Peace is the truth for all who behold themselves as a part of the Great One. He that solves to be man within the skin shall possess the will that each one is given in the fulfillment of the Great One in the endeavors of physical manifestation. The water bearer shall bring to us the sound of new life. We hear the music as it floats upon our skies. We hear the drumming as the sounds penetrate the Earth. We feel the beat that returns to us from within the Earth. We know we are the ones who shall bring the body into the stage of peace. Our works shall be known and acted upon by the living and loving gods of this universe. We share our thoughts with whomever shall have the ears to listen and the hearts to understand.

Our forefathers rested in this place to establish an island of total love and compassion. We know ourselves to be of this Earth yet part of the great scene that plays itself upon firmament. Our knowledge has been built upon our reserves that were placed here thousands of years before to help lift us from our own demise. We rise up into the knowing that all is here to be realized. We are the great beings and our strength is in this knowledge. We go forth in our lives with the anticipation that all life is in balance, in concordance to the One.

Our friends from the great star-ships come and share their life stories. We listen with utmost fascination. We know that multiple lives exist everywhere on this world as well as others. We surrender to this knowing because all lives everywhere are so intertwined. Our lives come together for the betterment of all. Our friends' stride in their knowledge of science, in architecture is most fascinating. It helps us understand our world. We learn from each other. We look forward to the day when we all can live together in one place to achieve total harmony of our worlds. We are not at that place where our physical selves can combine into an even greater being. So we continue to share what we have learned.

Our main source of knowledge comes from our being able to hear and feel all vibrations. We know that when these vibrations solidify, then they become solid or physical where we can see them with our physical eyes. We delight in our experiments as our world grows with new life. We have found that this new life can reproduce itself within its own particular vibration. Many of our beings help with our foods, the tilling of the lands. Some have great strength that our human form does not. We have worked with these beings for their strong backs and keen eye sight *(horses)*. Others help with keeping the soils loose for the growing of our foods. We take within our being those leafy plants and berries. These help keep our forms strong especially when there are extreme changes in our atmosphere.

We share our knowledge only with those who hold these as truths and share equally with all others. We honor all who live with this peace. With this declaration, we invite others in the stars to share with us to bring about new life to be explored and born in the great field of matter, the physical we so much enjoy. Knowledge brings us new understanding of all life. We know that all possibilities exist in this realm and those realms that we cannot yet see but feel.

The beat of this Earth resides in the heavens with the beats of all worlds. They are one heart beat and are called the Great One. We are peace and we live in truth.

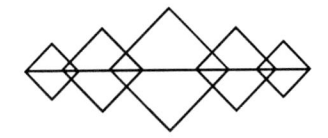

Q – *Who is the water bearer?*

A – The water bearer is the constellation of Orion, Sirius, and the Pleiades.

Q – *Do the Monrovian Beings exist today on this earth?*

A – The ones you call the Asians who live in the mountains of Tibet are remnants of this civilization.

January 5, 2004

(32)

Story of Heaven Eleven

This is a story about a ship that eventually wrecked. Brave men and women were aboard this ship to sail to new parts of the world before it was turned into ice. Their sights were on new land that would help replenish their foods for the anticipated Ice Age. An unusual tribe they were. Their remnants are located in the New Zealand area today.

Men of old recited that they would return to these parts of the world to bring about a stabilization of the tectonic plates of the Earth. Thus we call in the age of stabilization or the spreading of the ice. The ice shall help level the crust of this earth to bring about a balance in the waters and the lands

Our task is to find land that will grow all of our needed foodstuffs to store while we wait out the decimation of the high lands to bring balance to the lower lands. We search for the rich clay that nurtures plants into foods that can be stored in their dry state. This clay is known to have the properties that enrich the plants with nutrients that give added strength to the human body. Our animals shall be a base of warmth and guidance once we find the new land. They shall assist with the planting, the irrigation, and the harvest of the plants.

We call upon the Father, the stars in heaven that shall be our focus as we cross the seas. They shall be as our guides to where we shall land and start the harvest. We have brought along a multitude of seeds that shall be the basis for the first feed. The seeds from this initial harvest shall be the basis for the next generation of fruits. This shall continue until we see that the stars have lined up to tell us that it is time for the great Ice Age. We know of the forthcoming Ice Age from the messages of the Star People. We know of our duties and what we must produce for the populace of this planet. We know of the internal rumblings of this Earth and they manifest themselves in the outer shell of the planet. We accepted this task with our communications with the Star People that we call the Council of Nun. Should our task not be completed, then the people of this world will perish and a new people will be brought here to start another race.

Our seal is on the sides of our ship. We are called the Heaven Eleven. We embrace our duties as our commitment to the One God, the holy waters of eternal life. We shall land in the new world to continue our race. Our ship is ready to sail. The winds blow from the east. It is time. The words of our eternal God is "Ye shall go unto the untamed waters and find that life is everywhere. You are that life and you are everywhere. Know this in your travels."

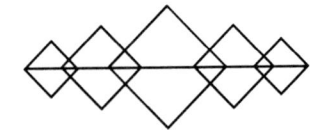

Q – Please explain more about the Council of Nun?

A – The Council of Nun are beings who make up the trio *(the third eye)* of Bath Kol *(Hebrew meaning "the voice of the Dove" – the power activating the feminine side of creation)*. Their numbers signify the life and death of forms. They are in the structures of every single cell of all living matter. They are you and every being who lives on the earth plane.

According to the Metaphysical Bible Dictionary, Unity School of Christianity, 1966: In Chronicles 7:27, Non – Nun in Hebrew. Spreading abroad; becoming extended; prolific; continuous; posterity; eternal increase; interpenetrating all; fish.

Nun signifies the great and continuous increase of Truth, of spiritual ideas, in the consciousness of the individual who opens his heart and mind to the Truth and wills to do the will of God, to keep the divine law.

March 29, 2004

The Ides of March

The Ides of March was a calling for those who were ready to enter into the new Kingdom. It was a calling forth of those souls who would brave the inefficiencies of the rulers of the day. They were told to remove their masks, to be true to themselves and their beliefs. This was a turning point in Europe.

Let it be known that man shall march on to the truths of the divine. We will sit no longer and abide by the rules that do not serve us. We will prevail. Let no man tell you that you cannot become that which you are to become. Let no man tell you that you are obligated to do something that is against your being. Let no man argue against this great cause. Let it be known that we stand tall and will not move from our sacred place.

We are here to serve all of humanity. We know of our divine rights. The anarchy that is in place shall fall on its own because it serves no one but those who rule. We march for the truths to be revealed. We know ourselves to be the commoner yet in the eyes of God, we are Man. We pursue the right to be self-governed. We are peace and all men are created equal, so only peace can be. We stretch ourselves to become the new pillars of strength, of dignity, of reward. For reward is in the heart. Peacefully we march on to our paths of righteousness. No evil shall come upon us.

God of Abraham, we know that all truth lies in your bosom. We beseech you to shower your love and guidance so we will follow the path of good. Great are they who shall heed your love. We travel on to the corners of this Earth. You are the ruler of all and we will follow what is good, what is peace, and what is love.

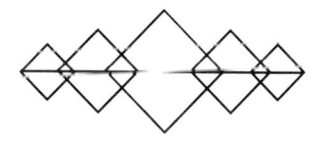

Per the *World Book Encyclopedia, 1988 Edition:*

In the old Roman calendar, the Ides was a day near the middle of each month. It was the 13th of all months except March, May, Judy, and October, when the Ides fell on the 15th. The Ides of March, on which Caesar was assassinated, was March 15.

May 23, 2004

Book of Geldeiah

There comes a time that needs to be spoken in a language that is easy to understand and interpret. This book deals with the time when humankind was at a brink of extinction because of the fallibility of the star men that came here to rescue man. Man did not need to be rescued and so it was learned that man indeed was a specimen that was created to continue the powerful life force of the universe. When it became known that the species of man contained this powerful life force, then many civilizations came to this land to learn, to capture, to interpret how this force worked and why it was so strong to make man into hu-man.

The forces of the gods have been felt in this earth. This round sphere was created from the break up of the temporal dynasty of the lords of nations. These lords grew in their responsibilities that they would become the inhabitants of the spheres of nations. In their knowledge of the star systems that speak of time within time, they thought that stars would be breached and resurrected in the name of the holy one of old. Within the spectrum of the laiz, it was determined that the gentle force of life would be embedded within the spectrum of this corner of the heavens. This universe would represent thought as the originator. It is the spark of masterhood, just one aspect of many universes.

The knowledge that was put forth contained life in its propagation of light, the gentle force of Love. This Love activated within itself extended life. This life grew to include all thought within itself. It became the activator and activatee. It consumes itself in order to understand itself. This great force of love is the energy that is with no beginning and no end. It is the all and absolute yet carries within itself the ability to become the novature of future timelines and zones.

We come to the point that all is to be in its own right and its own force. What brings the eloquence of this mission to the forefront of many civilizations is the ability to transcend the encumbrances bestowed upon the peoples and the lands. Truth about the worlds, where they are in their evolutions, their connections within the life force, the continuation of life without the knowledge that all is in an order of progression, is but a part of the mission. Remembrances of times past and times future have created the new world. Bring about justice, of love of all life. Existence is more than what is/has been realized. It is Life. It is the spark that moves within itself to create more sparks, aspects of itself. It moves in such a manner as to evoke new ways of Being. This mission is to bring about a finale of worlds in chaos. No more will the light be suffocated. It will burst forth and out and will consume the darkness. It will not fail as there is no such memory that failure even exists.

Those who hold the lighted forces, come into this arena. Make yourselves known. Be the conduits of light. Steady your own forces. Bring about the will of divine love. You are called here to assimilate all forces so that you will know all shades of the light. You shall experience a newness about yourself. Know that you shall be guided by your own forces. All the forces shall combine into one Love, for that is where they all came from. Know your light and know what you have before you.

The divine spark is you in your motion, your movement of the love in action. Gratitude to this wonderful light parade. Be ready to take your positions. You each are given all the divine assistance you require. We honor you in your love, in the torch that you carry. Stand firm in your light and you shall always remember that you have come from your greatness. Move out into the galaxies of new. Your personal worlds await your return. We will stand ready to be at your side when necessary at your request. We will not and cannot interfere without your asking. Life, this force of Love, is your heart. Connect to it at all times and your missions shall be much easier. Blessings rain on you. Feel them with every step, every decision that you make. The fleet stands ready to move you into position.

We are One, there is no other. All worlds rejoice at this moment as the worlds close together in utmost love and respect of all life. May you find it in your heart to hear the thoughts that shall permeate all the worlds in the soft glow of love.

Peace Be to all nations. Rise and begin your missions. It shall begin.

We of the Galactic Council salute you all. Me se cum lo. In obedience to the One, we sign off.

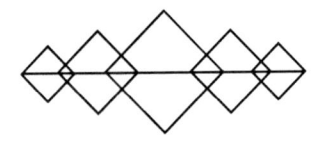

Q – Why is this book named Book of Geldeiah? Who or what is Geldeiah?

A – Geldeiah is the name of the third civilization of this earth. They also colonized the other planets within your solar system. In the 4th century of the time period known to you as predinosaur, there existed groups of beings, each having their own set of priorities in their missions. Some were the "cave" people while other settled here from distant star systems. Geldeiah refers to these beings from distant star systems.

Q – What is the "spectrum of laiz"?

A – Within the abilities of the Godhead, are all things possible. Nothing can interfere with this process.

Q – What does the term "novature" mean?

A – Novature means to make new. It is the culmination of the eruption or nova.

Q – This book is very powerful in its message. Is there more that can be said about this book?

A – Greetings! It is I, the Master of new creation. I reside in each and every one of you who read of these words. I am a part of this whole. You are in this process of thought manifestation. This, indeed, is the mission of love in its highest form. I honor all of you for your courage in your endeavors to produce a life of peace, harmony, and abundance. You are the glory of all civilization.

November 23, 2003

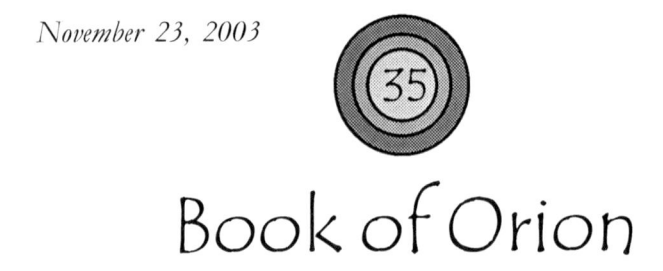

Book of Orion

It was the night before the storm when the oceans' inhabitants made a rush to safety, their survival. They watched as the waters swayed to and fro. They knew their world was to become vastly different. This story is about the forces that came to this planet to start another race, another time frame. They brought with them technologies that are being tapped into this day. The actions left in writings and figures in the deep seas will give humanity a glance of what was once this planet. Those beings from Orion came to join the other races and species to make their statement, their ideas of what creation is and should be. Their intellect is far greater than those who had already colonized this planet. They helped create a new form, new life, in their image. They were called the Gods of Abraham.

To man, those inhabitants of this planet. We find thee a prisoner of your own making. We shall release those bondages that have held you in this realm. You have flourished yet you do not know why. You have come to break the commandments that were given to hold you in bondage. We come to be of assistance to bring you into the new way of life, the new way of being.

We acknowledge you as divine beings brought to this edge of the galaxy to continue life in the image of the most magnificent One. We are the makers of a new image. Our planetary system is made up of one thousand planets. Our position in the heavens gives us the ability to oversee other creations that are plentiful in this area of the cosmos. Our demeanor is to rally those who will carry the divine seeds, those beautiful ones who shall inherit the worlds. Our attributes in this area shall continue until all is in concordance to the divine plan of this universe. Our job will be complete when this is done.

We bring to you our great ones who shall be as teachers and soothsayers. They shall impart knowledge that a kingdom beyond this earth does exist and shall overcome all dark forces that come between the earth peoples and ourselves. We shall show the peoples that all power is available to all ones who will live the divine laws. Our promise is to continue all assistance until the day when man can rule himself. Our body of humanity shall share all knowledge and wisdom and these shall pass down into the ages. Our commitment has been made. Our most magnificent one, Lord Maitreya, shall be the overseer of this plan. He brings with him the wisdom and knowledge of this whole universe. He knows of the total divine plan that has been put into place. He shall not surrender this job until all is done. To be able to meet this plan is the job of Osiris, Lord and master of disguise, yet touches the very heart of all living beings. We exist for the One, the One Force of this Universe.

The events that shall come to pass have been decided with the earth's inhabitants making the final decisions. Man in his state of Light are the ones who have the final say on how he will progress. With the realization that man, indeed, has made his own decisions with guidance from our command, we shall move on to assist man in his new creations in far-away galaxies. We will combine our efforts, our knowledge, and our technologies, as we move on into the heavens.

Our seed shall be a part of this great change. Our seed shall be as pure luminescent light that shall lock itself within the souls of man. Our light shall be as a blending of divine energies into the new seeds. Man will know himself as the Seeds of Abraham, ones of gladness.

All flora and fauna shall also know of themselves as great powers to bring balance to the nature kingdoms that already exist here. They shall tap into the energy vortices that make up the atmosphere of this beautiful planet. They ride the waves of divine regeneration using the power that is inherent in their making. Ones who came before us, the Venovians, already had set up this magnificent nature kingdom. Other civilizations who had also come here and then left, brought with them their own nature powers that have continued, and, in most instances, co-exist with the newer flora and fauna.

This world, this beloved planet with the heart of Gaia, shall become the Star of On. It is One with all of the Universe, yet One within Herself. The Seeds of Abraham shall flourish and bring the New Age of living within the heart of Creator. The love of all life shall be our guidance. We are one with All. We are the Gateway to living with the divine plan. We are and will do no less than live in Love.

August 19, 2002

Book of Isaiah

Sananda and I stand on a rocky slope of the mountains in Brazil. We are on a ridge that runs north and south and is positioned toward the western boundary of Brazil. Here many civilizations of the past lived in these rugged parts to work with the energies of Albaktan, an ancient civilization before the time of Lemuria or Mu.

The sign of the egg, of reproduction. We bring to you activation of the energy center of the humanoid body that deals with reproduction. The cervix of the female shall have within glands that stimulate a mucous to carry the seed of a male. We have perfected the division of the egg and in order for that egg to be nourished, it must pass through the canal into the womb where it can implant itself to the walls. The development of this area of the body is to hone into the energies of the "B" plane of existence. This honing device shall be as a cursor to move into the function mode of copulation. The stimulus of the pineal gland shall activate the adrenal glands of the male penis to project itself into the female. The heightened state that is induced by the stimulation of the glands brings about a release of endorphins. The energy exchange between the male and female partners sends a vibration into the void to call upon a spirit soul to embody into a human form. An exchange has been made with both the partners and the new seed to carry out the divine plan of this planet.

With this new seed shall be brought additional "family" to protect and communicate as the seed comes into physical being. The function of the "family" is to develop the seed or being into the body that the entity needs to fulfill his or her mission while in embodiment. They bring the necessary impulses or energy to the growing seed by working with the mother or female that has produced the egg.

The process of protosynthesis enables the developing body to respond to these impulses by applying an overtone of electromagnetic bands of stimulus to compose the structure into the physical. The structure of groups of life begin to categorize themselves into round life forms that cling together into shapes held by this electromagnetic force. The new life form divides itself with the memory of the crystals that make up the filaments making up their own magnetic force. The streams of life force energy are taken from the void of all potential. This transference feeds upon itself until the structure can no longer hold the energy with the structure collapsing upon itself. The mind of Creator, that liquid light or intelligence, shall connect into this new being at the moment that the structure is to be separated from within the womb of the female. The filaments that comprise memory shall be as recorders for energy vibrations or impulses (data collectors) of the bodies experiences of emotions. During the life stream of that body, there will be synapses of former and/or future data being retrieved. This is to bring into the fullness of being in the physical. The whole of the Being shall then release itself into the white energy or mind of Creator to develop other ways of being. Thus the structure shall be as a tool of Creation.

The memory of consciousness shall remain in the vestiges of time rolled into the Great Central Sun of All That Is. Man shall be as the Great Creator from whom all things are made possible in the flesh of the body. The dimensions of all man shall be as a conduit unto the civilizations of those universes that vibrate beyond that which is seen in the lower or more dense creations. Man shall continue in this physical to fully understand what being a creator is. When there is no more need and the energy reaches a vibration that exceeds that which can be made physical, then that energy shall go on to the nitreal form bringing the wisdom of being man. All is then greater because of this. So be it!

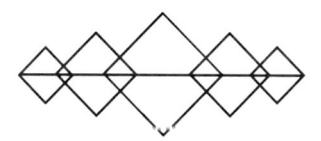

Q - Explain the "energies of Albaktan."

A – This refers to the concourse of events before those beings came in and settled into the regions of Lemuria. The energies were different than they are today in that the earth was in a much more gaseous and water form. These beings who lived in that era worked the waters as their living homes.

Q – What is the "B" plane of existence?

A – The physical part of your reality.

Q – Per my dictionary, one of the functions of the adrenal glands, attached to the kidneys, have three important functions, one of them being that the adrenal glands produce small amounts of sex hormones, chiefly the male hormones called androgens. The adrenal androgens help regulate the development of pubic hair and other early sexual characteristics in both males and females during the period just prior to puberty.

What is this book saying that the adrenal glands have a much grander purpose in reproduction?

A – The adrenal glands indeed do have a much grander purpose. Scientists, start researching the connections of the pineal gland and the adrenals during the period of copulation.

Q – What is the process of protosynthesis?

A – Creation in an archetype or a prototype form. In this usage, a physical being.

Q – What is the meaning of the word "nitreal"?

A – Nonphysical form.

When channeling the above book, I "saw" this symbol for Albaktan:

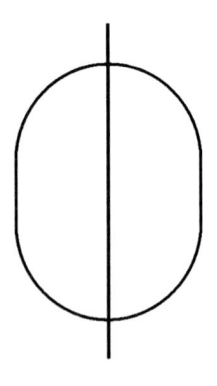

August 29, 2002

Book of the Rainbow

    Sananda and I stand in the Valley of Peace, which is located between two mountains, which are part of a chain of islands in the Pacific Ocean that are called Fiji Islands. This particular island is the largest in the southwest part of the chain. We stand next to a roaring stream cascading down from the mountain springs. There are small villages of natives scattered about. These people are very wise to the energies of the mountains and can sense life within their bellies. They consider these mountains to be alive, to have a soul. I sense that there are tunnels and large caverns in these mountains left there by a large civilization that once inhabited that area when it was a much larger piece of land or continent. These people were a very gentle people who loved to work with the earth. They became great botanists and have left their legacy in the caverns. They came to earth approximately one million years ago and their wisdom will soon be felt throughout the earth.

    Sananda speaks: **"There is an energy here I have not felt before."**

    I saw Sananda's eyes become a whitish light blue like a bolt of electricity shoot through him. He looked very uncomfortable. Then two entities (masters) worked from both sides of his crown chakra to help stabilize him. This area needs a balancing of energies. We face one another with our fingers touching as we send balancing energies into the earth in this area. There is a large rock that holds much information. Some of this energy may have been tampered with, but with the balancing energies, the memory stored in the rock is returning to the way it was left by the ancient ones of millennia past.

Fusion of the molecular bodies of the great white spring of the language of light shall become manifest in the earth made of the ten elements of matter to be introduced into the time/space portal of condensed light. Two cells combine to form a new section of matter that shall separate into cones for new seeds. All is connected by the filament strands of photon energy emanating from the star nucleus of the planetary bodies of Sagittarius. These shall form clusters that divide by their own power and by the light of the photon. The mouth of the cavity left by the separation of the "seed" shall absorb the mucual energies of the forces of the Heman[1]. A rod of silver light will break forth through this interaction, and a new form shall emerge to co-exist with the separated seed.

The combination of seeds shall become as the basis of the floral kingdom that shall flourish on the new planet. They shall enter into the domain of the new land. The elements that make up water - hydrogen and oxygen - shall be as the facilitator of growth, the body of the plant. Water shall become as the builder, mover of the conel seeds. These seeds shall lay their base within the land and waters where they can hold their structure upon the land and draw their nourishment from the elements. As they absorb the elements, they shall gather strength within their structure. The mix of the nutrients absorbed into this new body will be a conduit of energy into the atmospheres that surround the planetary structure. The breath of man shall draw upon the release of oxygen and nitrogen from the leaves and stems. These live structures shall reach heavenward in much abundance. These shall become as food for the fowl and for the animals.

This new species will be as a cover of the land. We introduce the floral for its beauty and its ability to speak of the conditioning of the soil, the matter in which the seeds are nurtured to send their roots to hold the waters and the stability to hold the structure that emerges above the earth's crust. Each structure creates its own rhythm, its communication to the other structures and to the other beings that reside in and on the earth plane.

We shall continue creating new designs; species that will better serve man and animal. The knowledge that has been recorded into the archives of the ancients, before humankind, will be released unto man, those who are ready for the determination of the holy vows of the Creator in the making of the new creators within the hemisphere of form. And in so doing shall the opportunity to create creatures, all life shall be brought forth and multiplied in the realm of slowed enigmatic waves of light onto the spheres that share their beings. The decree has been made and it is so!

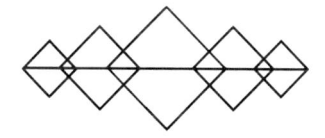

1 Heman – from the Metaphysical Dictionary by Unity: Thoughts full of trust in God – honest, true, steadfast, accurate. Also thoughts of the intellect, rather than of Spirit, since the wisdom of Solomon, spiritual wisdom, greatly excelled the wisdom of Heman.

Q – Please define Heman.
A - The forces of love (or God) that blend the energies of the earth into the energies of the God Force, a plan of physical creation. Without the God Force, the weakened state of the Heman dies and the energies are reabsorbed into the Temple of Solomon – the void of all existence but from where all things flow.

The symbol I "saw" is:

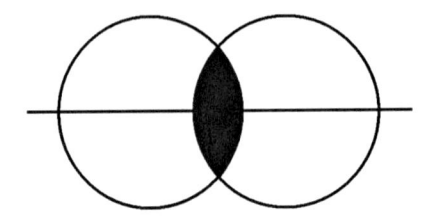

This book speaks of the above shaded area.

September 6, 2002

Book of the Journey

Sananda and I stand in the northern part of Africa in that country known as Tunisia. Here were left remains of a race of beings who came to this earth to leave their gift of changing or transmuting matter from one state into another. They used this area as an example: the land was desert like and within a few revolutions (days and a day refers to a thousand years) of the planet, plant life appeared. All was lush as a beautiful garden. This book deals with how this transformation was accomplished.

The tablets on which this book is transcribed are located on the plains north of the Raditon Mountains of Tunisia. There a plateau exists where these people lived. They gained much of their energy to procreate from the crystal plate that makes up this plateau.

September 9, 2002

Matter is energy made up of photon light beams arranged in a pattern of love. We, the Rasputens, use our creative energy to rearrange molecules. We can change life with just our thoughts. Our concentration must be so focused that all our being radiates out a signal that calls in life from the cosmos, void, All That Is.

The earth is made up of living, breathing life. It is malleable, transferable, and transmutable, as long as the inner body of this loving planet is not tampered with. Within this great planet are the life forces that give this sphere her living body. She, too, is able to move within her shell, change her shell, both the inner and outer shell. She is grand in her beingness, therefore we cannot touch that part of her being which she is totally in control of. We concentrate our creative powers on her outer shell only. We are the form givers. Our creations can be seen in all the physical dimensions. Our intent has been to assist our brothers and our sisters in creating life that is hospitable to them, a temple for them to work from, to work with in creating their creations.

We have a great love for the human. The human themselves are magnificent beings with unlimited powers to create with the hands and heart of the God force. We work with the humans in setting up an energy field, a field in which they can do their greatest works.

We have set up centers of great power using the pulsing electro/magnetic waves of the clear crystal bodies set into the mineral kingdoms already in the earth's crust. These powerful entities are put here in abundance at key intersections from which the life force of the planet breathes. This crystal is a gift from ourselves and those from the sixth galaxy. The planets in the sixth galaxy are made up of sparkling crystalline structures. They glow with all colors as their prisms reflect the great light within the planets themselves. Our job is to give mankind the tools of these magnificent crystalline structures to manifest wonders of pulsating and vibrating life.

We will gladly assist mankind, once he is the vibration of total love, create different forms of matter. We can create life in its simplest form (the cell) and vibrate its being into dividing itself into form. We can program the cell to be any form of plant that we desire. Then this plant is given the ability to procreate itself into more selves. This life force is perpetuating. Our knowledge of the plant kingdom comes from our own planet which is filled with "balls" of light with an iridescent quality bouncing and floating over the surface. These most wondrous beings (the iridescent balls) form a complex web of interactive protons and neutrons set within a spin of electrons. These protons and neutrons can be repositioned to form other matter. Our thoughts projected into the web are what reposition them. Therefore it is through our concentrated thoughts that we can transform all matter. Our impulses radiating from our beings into the waves of the spin of the electrons, moves the protons and neutrons to their new positions. The energy from the crystals assists us in our thoughts. They are magnifiers. We can move mountains as well as grow tiny blades of grass with only our thoughts.

Our mission is to aid mankind in the manifestation of new creations using our technology. We offer our guidance in love and ask that only love be used for all creation. From our hearts to the heart of this grand sphere, we look forward to our merging of minds for the new adventure. We will be ready with open hearts when all of mankind have their hearts open to receive this love. With this quiver, we write this message as our invitation into the advanced world of matter. Cum shi di au pume.

Can you see yourselves as the writers of these words? Soon your remembrances will emerge. You will remember that you wrote of these days to come. The days are here. Wake up mankind and look at your creations. Reach into your hearts and hear the beat of the drums as they call you to your past and future. Remember, you are here now to remember.

All of the glory of heaven is at your disposal. It is here and now. You ask of the chaos that is going on in this world? With chaos comes change. Your world is changing, you are changing. We leave you at this moment with these words: "Cherish what you create and your world will again be heaven, your Garden of Eden."

October 2002

Book of Genes

Today there is much talk about genes, what they are and how they affect everyone on this planet. This book was written at the turn of the structure that you know as moon. The moon gravitates on an axis.

Please explain.

Your moon came into being shortly after the Earth, or, more appropriately, when Lady Gaia asked for assistance to help stabilize her orbit in this solar system. Your moon has a core of heavy yet molten iron with a strong magnetic pull. Within the very center of the core is another body of light crystal that acts as the generator for the stabilization of Lady Gaia. This creates a mechanism for the human body to power their own magnetic forces within the body. These can be found within the genetic structure. This book deals with this operation.

Can you explain more about how all of this came about?

This will be explained in a future book.

Thank you.

A magnetic clock exists within the body structure. The main controls are located within the brain stem called the medulla oblongata. Each cell produced in the body is coded with a system of rectangles and squares intertwined so as to make up cross axis's that create polarities *(as above so below)*. In the periphery of each rectangle and square is a substance of crystal *(same makeup as the crystal in the moon)* that filters the polarities into action. Each rectangle and square turn on their own individual axis and spin through their axial counterparts. Within the crystal walls are the divine codes or energies that link the human body to all of the universe. This turning on the axis is what holds the cells together in a magnetic bond. When that bond is broken, the cell releases its energy into the crystal of the new cell created from photosynthesis, a mirror-like creation.

The bond of the human body corresponds to the magnetic energies of Lady Gaia, your moon, as well as the positioning of the stars and planets seen and unseen. All life has a push and pull effect. The human body then shall be a composite of the forces of the four planetary systems that control this side of the universe within the confines of physical form. This bond can be broken when the velocity of the cells increase due to the release of the strong magnetic pull. Within the structure of the atom, the life force of physical creation, are the spins of electrons. These atoms, in turn, create a universe within a universe. They are what make up the body crystal and can be manipulated into other forms.

The central processing center, the magnetic clock or medulla oblongata, is connected to the life force of All That Is or the magnetic rod of all existence. This connection rod of energy, when activated, can change the force field of the body and send it into a less dense frequency of vibration (a faster spinning of the rectangles and squares) that shoot out sparks of vineral energy into the All That Is. This gives the body a new place of being and a new set of parameters from which the intellect and heart can experience.

Our gift to this universe will be the ability to assist Lady Gaia, her inhabitants, and the human to access the higher energies for their own particular experience of the higher realms of existence. This book of knowledge is left here in the pyramid of communication and higher consciousness at the center of the outgoing vortex of this planetary body.

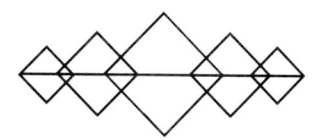

Q - Can this book be found?

A - *Only when it is "time." There is more to this book than just the words. This book is an actual crystal form.*

Q - Who are these beings?

A - *They come from the planetary system of Arcturus under the auspices of the Sirian High Council.*

Q – Please explain "vineral energy"?

A – Vineral energy is that energy which is produced by the human body through its association with the crystal energies of this planet. It is what connects you to the divine of All That Is. Once this association is understood is when man will find the crystals that have been hidden.

March 24, 2003

Book Of Illumined Truth

Upon the stage is a theory of basic light which encompasses the vibrational frequencies of the human genome. These people brought to this land the knowledge that is being looked at today with awe and wonder of the universe in its smallest aspects.

The beginning of time is nothing more than the mixture of the Holy Grail of life with the mechanism of light in its rainbow of colors and frequencies. Color can be divided in many spectra of frequencies that emit a vibration that stimulates the molecules that make up this part of the universe. These stimulations are to enhance the quality of the molecular or biological forms by the movement of ions to create a patterning of rapid sequences of color. This is what is seen by the human eye. By the slowing of the movements will the human express themselves in the physical to encode the Earth Mother with the decibels of sound to hold her together in the rapid movements of the universe.

The out-breath of the God Force pushes the forms into being on the plane of existence. The in-breath releases the light body to move freely about. This movement gives the soul the quantum leap to co-create in all worlds.

Mystery of the Universes

The force that is governed is the mind of Creator by the splitting of the duties inherent in this part of creation. When the Council of Five released their vision of the cosmos of the triad of the universes, the call went out (sound vibrations) into the void (or space of possibility) to fulfill the desire to create a bastion of new life in the format of biological connections. The biology of form was thus introduced.

You, the creators, are here to be. You are to be in physical form as well as in light body. Your bodies shall intertwine in this matrix of creation. You shall know the matrix by the movement of energy in your bodies. Recognize the juncture of the paradigms within each of you.

This book of knowledge is to be held by the initiates and protected until the time of tribulation. The tribes shall merge into a consciousness of the One.

This book is part of a series that exists in the Great Hall of Records, those books left in the ethereal realms by yourselves. Blessed love is given to you by the Council of Five. Adonai.

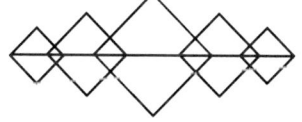

Q – Please explain the out-breath of the God Force as well as the in-breath.

A – The out-breath is the sending out or call from Creator. It is dividing oneself. It is the thought. The in-breath is the release of Creator in its creations/co-creators.

Q – What are the duties inherent in this part of creation?

A – You, as creator, are in a light body as well as a biological body. Therefore you create in both bodies. This is your duty as creator.

March 3, 2003

Book of Blue

Across the horizon is a magnificent blue that fills the body with a tender feeling of awe. Have you wondered about this experience? Your expression "clear as blue" has more meaning than you may be aware of. This book deals with the blue ray of hope, good health, and divine imagery. This book was written approximately 12,000 years ago along the Aegean Sea. Its author is a civilization that studies the twelve rays. They have since exited this planet. They are the group known as the great scientists, the Algers.

Around this fabulous planet exists an atmosphere made up of gases that appear as blue to the eye. The gases stimulate planet growth of the plant kingdom as well as the animal kingdoms. Within this gaseous mixture lie the photons[1] that hold the gaseous particles together in a fashion that forms a ring around the planet herself. Her waters take in some of these gases with the addition of elements that nourish the planet. Her waters bathe her in a substance that breathes or pulses with the push and pull of the magnetics that are within her, the moon, and the planets, particularly the Sun. The iron content that helps hold the planet into a round sphere pulls on the ions[2] and holds the moisture in the air or atmosphere of the planet.

The blue ray, whose wavelength stretches into the outer realms, connects the various planetary structures to form a grid. This grid enables the star beings to travel the cosmos in an efficient manner.

Beyond the spectrum of the visible rays is an energy of ultraviolet that is used to disseminate the forces of the various dimensions that reside on and in this planet. The blue ray traverses all dimensions in its ability to detect the beat and pulses of the universe in every sphere of existence. It is the ray of clarity that brings a likeness to all dimensions for communications.

Discussion of the remainder of the spectrum is within the family of Job, the one who leaves his mark on the synthesis of matter and antimatter. Blue will remain as that conductor of plasma[3] into the many forms of creation.

The night shall become the day. For in the light shall all man be born in the memory of the Father, the Father of all existence.

The meaning of the word "Father" is Source.

Q – *Please explain more about this book.*

A – In our visible spectrum, violet has the shortest wavelength. Indigo next, then blue. Farther along the spectrum, the light has increasingly longer wavelengths with the longest wavelength of light that we can see appear deep red in color.

---

1 Photon – *The Living Webster Encyclopedic Dictionary of the English Language:* a quantum of electromagnetic radiation moving at the velocity of light with energy in proportion to its frequency.

2 Ions – *The Living Webster Encyclopedic Dictionary of the English Language:* an electrified atom or group of atoms, having either a positive or negative charge, which has increased or decreased in number of electrons after electrolysis (the decomposition of a chemical compound by an electric current)

3 Plasma – *The Living Webster Encyclopedic Dictionary of the English Language:* …an electrically charged gas occupying most of outer space beyond the earth's atmosphere.

Light waves are a form of electromagnetic waves which consist of patterns of electric and magnetic energy. The visible spectrum is only a small part of the electromagnetic spectrum – the entire range of electromagnetic waves. Beyond the violet end of the visible spectrum are ultraviolet rays, x-rays, and gamma rays.

Color within your visible spectrum reflect the sounds of the Universe. In each dimension the sounds/colors change with the increased velocity of atoms. However the blue, indigo, violet rays continue into all dimensions because of their shorter wavelengths which travel faster along grid lines.

More knowledge of color and wavelengths will be covered in a future book.

May 11, 2003

Book of Letters

The world of writing began when man could no longer use his mind for open communication. Loss of this ability took man to where he had to write in symbols for mass communication. Early writings were pictographs, symbols of activities of the day. The symbols grew to have more meanings reflecting emotional states of being.

Numbers or integers have always been a way of communication even with telecommunication. Numbers were used in all areas of mathematics and science. Equations were written bringing a more intense vibrational quality to the ideas presented through eons of time.

Writing has been a science in and of itself. It gives the mind codes that are downloaded and processed for the evolvement of man since the loss of telecommunication. This book deals with this phenomenon, the beginning of written thought.

Communication has digressed to the point of verbal sounds. Sounds emitted through the larynx or main vibrational chamber within the physical body is the most effective form of communication with the dismissal of the third eye. Forms of top notch frequencies are the basis for understandings among man, animal, and plants. The cells of each of these bodies resonate to certain frequencies depending upon the state or divine resonance to all of creation.

Each sound or frequency has a corresponding symbol. These symbols derive their shapes from the vibrational qualities emitted or the shape or form of the atoms in molecular structure. Thus this written form of communication carries with it the sacred geometry of all existence.

Man is to use this form of communication until he reaches a point of knowingness that is within all of his cells. At that existence, he will no longer need most written communication except for some symbols that affect him deeply within. Until that time arrives, man is to use these symbols for the deliverance of thoughts. Manifestation shall take on another form because of this slow transference. Speech will become diverse as each individual receives this sound differently. The written symbols will change their shapes within the total matrix of codes. This will give man the chance to experience life in separation, the density of the gods of Abroc. Life will continue in this fashion until the hold of these ones is no longer useful and man advances to a higher state of consciousness. The towers that rise on the earth's surface will be as chambers that direct vibrational codes within this sphere to other spheres of like frequencies. The day of total harmonics will come again as all life including the life force of this sphere directs all thoughts to the total harmonics of Creator Sun. The letters of the harmonics *(musical notes)* will be the basis of the grids of life. Each species has their own song and all songs contribute to the harmonics of this sphere.

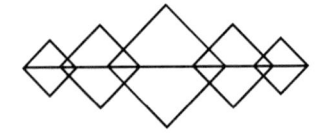

This book was written by the initiates of the Divine Centralles, those beings that have held the harmonics in place for the security of this planet. With love they share

their symbols with you. Their teachings will be found in the interior of this earth and within some of the structures such as the pyramids of Waitachoal.

The symbol shown to me:

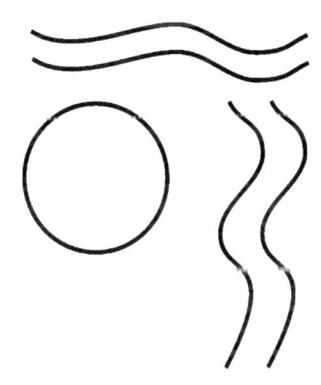

Q – Who are the gods of Abroc?

A – These were the peoples who had discovered this earth and her "sound." Scanning the Universe, they heard her (earth's) call. They responded and made earth their home. They are now known as the kings of Abraham, geneticists working with the biology of man.

Q – Where are the pyramids of Waitachoal?

A – These are located near the foothills of the Pyrenees, the mountain range between Spain and France.

Q – Can these pyramids be found?

A – The pyramids have eroded throughout the years as they are about one million years old. Their remnants do remain however. No, the building of these pyramids actually goes back approximately three million years.

June 1, 2003

Book of Gibraltar

The anatomy of mankind lies in the likeness of the forefathers of evolution. These beings brought their knowledge of the form into this state of awareness through the channels of the Lleken. These magnificent beings manifested their likeness into the third dimensional form to study how the form evolves as it accesses higher dimensions. Their knowledge was given to those beings who had an interest in the development of life on planet Earth. These books are located in the Archives of Iberashun, a great library that lies under the sea near the entrance into the Sea of Mediterranean.

Oh beautiful one of old, we bring you this knowledge, the form of man to grow and flourish on this planet Earth. This form shall vibrate to that of Earth. It shall traverse the magnetic fields with ease. It shall be able to hold the vibration of Lady Gaia. It shall be made of her elements. The love of the divine shall reside in each cell of the body.

The marriage of two bodies shall remake of themselves. One shall be as the proiator and the other the recipient. The form of the proiator shall sow the seed upon the appropriate moment the seed is ready to germinate. They shall copulate as one, intertwined in a matrix of divine union.

The form shall bear witness to all of creation. It shall have the knowledge that all creation is part of a much larger matrix of divine creation. The body shall float within the Earth's atmosphere. All movement is accomplished with the spark of electromagnetic energy flowing through all parts of the body. The appendages shall create with ease, legs for movement from one place to another, and arms to do more intricate tasks.

Nourishment to these appendages shall come through the flow of nutrients made up of particles that have a supreme consciousness. Its color shall be as the divine ray of love. This liquid (blood) shall pass through three mechanisms (organs) that shall cleanse it and keep it rotating through the system. Within this same system, shall this divine red liquid nourish the other organs. Man shall breathe the nutrients of Lady Gaia's breath. This dependency holds man and Earth together for the fulfillment of both divine creations. The breath of man shall take in these nutrients to bring in elements of nourishment.

The heart or pump of man shall be located in the central axis of the body. It holds the frequency of multiple dimensions. The mind contains the brain and the endocrine system. These systems connect the heart to the center of Creator, the thread of eternity. In the recesses of the brain are stored images on the crystal platelets. This gives man the ability to retrieve information. Also within the brain and glands is the ability to process and create new ideas, a co-creative process.

The beauty of the body is unsurpassed in its uniqueness. It is a similization of creators that have gone before with the ability to create new. We pass on this knowledge to continue the growth of wisdom within the will of Creator. With this text, details of each part of the body follows to explain its creation and function within the whole. The similitude of the body form is one of the grandest creations. It shall be used with the utmost care and gratitude of the divine.

Thank you, Great Creator, for our part in the development of the body. We shall observe its evolution as it resides in the seven rays, the third band wave of the twelve.

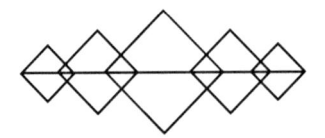

This book shall continue with its many parts. Understanding may be difficult to grasp but shall be studied by many in the healing professions.

The Endocrine System:

The endocrine system consists of glands that regulate body functions including regulating growth, the reproductive process, the way the body uses food, and helps prepare the body to deal with stress and emergencies.

The major endocrine glands include the adrenal glands, the pituitary gland, the parathyroid glands, the sex glands, and the thyroid gland. The brain, the kidneys, the stomach, and the pancreas also have endocrine tissues and produce hormones. The pituitary gland, which lies near the base of the brain, is often called the master gland. It releases a number of hormones, which, in turn, regulate other endocrine glands. However, the pituitary itself is controlled by hormones produced by the hypothalamus, a part of the brain. The hypothalamus links the nervous and endocrine control systems.

Q – I do not find the word "proiator"(pronounced pro-i-a-tor) in our dictionary. Please explain its meaning.

A – One that injects as the male into the female, the beginning of procreation.

Q – Please explain the last sentence of this book: "We shall observe its (the bodies) evolution as it resides in the seven rays, the third band wave of the twelve."

A – The seven rays are your rainbow or the colors red, orange, yellow, green, blue, indigo, and violet. The third band wave refers to the compass or direction of these seven rays. To try to put it into understandable terms – each color has a wavelength. Combined, the colors make white light. Your body contains all of these colors, yet you see one another with the colors separated. We see you as white light because we observe you in a higher dimension, a dimension without form, not the same as you physically observe your world (however, there are those on your earth plane who have this ability to see others without form). Therefore, the third band is that faction of the total that you see. There are many colors of creation that is beyond your abilities to see or even comprehend.

Q – You mention that the third band wave refers to the direction of the seven rays. What do you mean by direction?

A – Direction simply means the ability within your dimensional residence. As you ascend into the 4th and 5th dimensions, you will have a better understanding of this because you will witness new colors in your world.

There will be more books that are a continuation of this book. These books will be given for the next volume or compilation of books as this first volume is constructed.

Thank you.

June 9, 2003

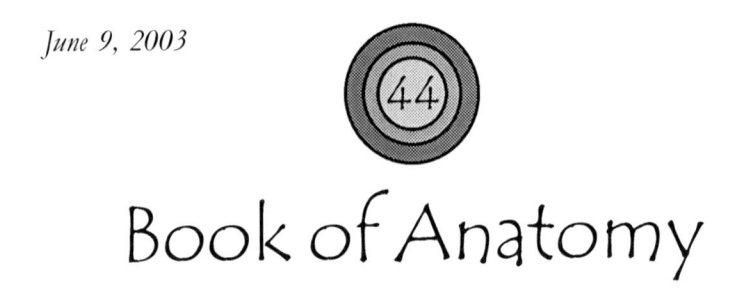

(44)

Book of Anatomy

This book is a summation of the texts of Ereocles, Greek God of Creation. These were written in the 4th century before my birth as Jesus.

The breath of life is in the filaments of the divine creation. It is made up of many liquid crystals. Each crystal holds a pattern of creation. This divine pattern is part of all of physical creation. Light enters each crystal matrix. The rays are distributed through this pattern and breathe a likeness to itself. The vibration of physical life occurs, all within this matrix of color. Each and every crystal builds on itself and is termed growth. This replication continues the species until such a moment, then the crystal is shaken by a new light, a new force of vibration. At that moment, all crystals change shape and leave off new patterns of creation.

The life form of the body which shall be called hu-man shall be a thought form (crystallized form) that is connected in its light prisms intersecting with the other light prisms of all created forms. The body hu-man shall be made of crystal patterns that resonate to the divine principles orchestrated from The Great Central Sun. The pathways of the lines of thought exist in a pattern that is reflected in each structure of each crystal. The memory or pattern of each crystal carries within it continuous life that traverses its structure to create movement. Within each crystal are smaller geometric patterns that resonate to the whole of the crystal as well as the forces of The Great Central Sun. This light permeation seeds the direct rays of illumination into more complex patterns. The patterns can be summed up as the five triangles that spin with the force of neutron energy upon the seed or nuclei of each crystal creating adam, the living co-creative force within this life system.

This sector of life is only one part of a whole matrix of various combinations of crystals that create other life forms. Movement within this form that the hu-man inhabit was created to understand the equivalent of creation within creation. The hu-man seed was developed to be constructors of new creation. The intelligent mechanisms placed within the crystals continues thought (light) from the directives of the larger matrix, The Great Central Sun. The Great Central Sun is a matrix itself. It contains a never-ending spectrum of color and vibration. Therefore, Creation is and continues as infinity. It is eternal.

The hu-man matrix was conceived by the out-pouring of love, a circular vibration of light. The hu-man shall be able to exist in multiple light frequencies. They shall create form within form. The intelligent structures shall create movements within themselves, their bodies of light. The power of light shall be the force of this creation. All light is the Supreme Being.

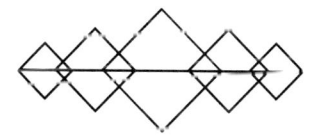

Q – Please explain neutron energy.

A – The atom contains a dense nucleus of neutrons and protons with the nucleus surrounded by a cloud of electrons. The atoms within the human body work with centrifugal force, like a ball swinging out on a string when held by a hand. This force causes a reverberation and ripples out into other atoms within the body. You then have movement from cell to cell. Neutrons in and of themselves have no charge, yet when paired with protons, a powerful force exists. Removing neutrons from the atom changes the complexity of the atom as it becomes less dense. However, the neutrons are then a powerful force on that cell which causes the nuclei to decay, giving off radiation. The atom then becomes radioactive in that the energy produced cannot be contained within the atom. When this energy is not released, then there is an explosion (or implosion), much like your atomic bombs, an implosion of particles.

What happens with the body is a continuation of thought or frequencies that make up all condensed matter, the frequencies causing the implosion upon the crystal platelets into other crystalized forms. They are programmed geometries, programmed by the Creator force/the individualized light body, which makes up the whole of All That Is. The human is constantly changing its form, the co-creative process.

June 16, 2003

○ 45 ○

Book of Zep Tepi

This book about Zep Tepi or First Time will bring humanity's consciousness to the time of remembrance when the mind energy was brought into alignment with the Holy Alcyone. This gateway to the higher intelligence of thought manifestation was instigated by the thought forms from the seed race of Orion. They brought to this earth the development of the seed into a Gematrian Body of Light. This body has transformed into the lower body called the seeds of Avalon.

The mind of Orion is the basis for this writing. Seeded here within the confines of this spaceship earth are the remnants of other star systems that have come to this region to project their likeness into the space/time continuum that is to exist for the purpose of time integration of the moving spectrum of light. This light is to be the basis of the physical patterning of the new seed. Within this seed is the awareness embedded in the matrix of thought patterns of Alcyone. This connection shall form the basis for an evolving species to turn into itself, to know of itself. Any hindrance of this process shall redefine this process within their own evolution.

The moment of the tonal vibration made with five sets of neutrons placed within the atom shall produce a new set of species within the confines of regeneration of its own cells. This cell exists within the parameters of the divine sequence of five octaves of tonal vibration that shall bring into this divine seed the tone of multiple existences. The wave patterns established by these five octaves work themselves into the matrix called the five senses. This produces within a physical being the opportunity to feel life in the moment. All existence is the constant movement of the light spectrums. These are seen as bursts of light by the human eye. The cause and effect of sensory output is felt within each being. The turntable of the new species shall come when the spectrums of all light beings in their physical forms are in alignment with the divine source. New life springs forth and is a continuum of the basic seed. The deliverance of the seed is in the knowledge that all creation comes forth from the alliance of Alcyone as the center of pulse radiations.

Concurrent stoppages of life force upon the atom shall cause a breakdown in the matrix and cause implosion. The energy released from this implosion is reabsorbed into the Gematrian Body of Light and the five senses cease to exist. The Gematrian Body with the added energies from the former physical body is grander in its composition by the impulses received through the former five senses.

This brings a complexity to the evolving human in that life-times upon life-times in this physical brings to the whole another creation that mirrors the greater creation. The fusion of the physical with the divine spectrum releases a new knowledge for the benefit of the whole. The integration of the light body over the physical body coupled with the five senses is the catalyst of emotion brought into the light body. Mind and matter exist together. A new spectrum has been introduced. All of creation shall know of this plan. This new dimension sends the message of completeness to the source of Holy Alcyone. Our pleasure to issue this divine decree that the plan is in effect. Humble we are in this intercession of divine rays. This is the new beginning.

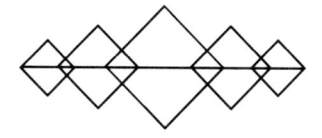

Q - Please further explain the Holy Alcyone.

A – The Holy Alcyone is a place which is also a state of mind in which the holy thought forms of All That Is are centered in this quadrant of this galaxy. Your galaxy rotates around this high-powered divine force.

Q – The last sentence of the first paragraph mentions that "any hindrance of this process shall redefine this process within their own evolution." Who or what is being referred to?

A – Any race of beings who tries to put a stop to this program will have to put into place a program of their own for their own evolution. This program has and will, in all probability, be stretched out to counteract the negative thought forms that went into trying to stop this program for planet Earth. Ones have come to "check out" this divine program to see if the advancements here can assist them in their own evolutions. A few beings have tried to take over this program but have failed. You, the divine humans on this Earth, will always be protected.

Q – Please explain the Gematrian Body of Light.

A – All human beings have a Gematrian Body of Light. This body is also known as your higher self or light body. It connects the human to the Christ Body Overself. It is a passage within the total self. Remember, within this book it says that mind and matter exist together. It is such a Divine Plan.

Human   Gematrian body surrounding the human   Alcyone or the Creative Mind encompasses all

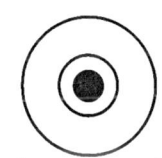

July 24, 2003

Book of Jerusalem

Time until now has been a searching, a searching for the divine. It is now that mankind is making the final decisions to be what the makers have intended since the mark of abstention was usurped onto the people of this planet. Release the old paradigm and step into the new. The clock is ticking. It is time!

This book details the true nature of what is Jerusalem. Besides being a city, the name Jerusalem implies a state of being. The book explains the rest.

The tendrils of biology have shifted to this Earth. The making of this body is in accordance to the making of the new human. The infrastructure of this new life form is a link to the map of the Nefilim. These beings who came to this part of the cosmos exercised their powers of co-creation in the making of mankind from the energies of the void. The non-form into the form is the description of the founders of this grand civilization. In bio-genesis, the form is made up of a network of synapses that relay information into the body structure from the outer body network of vast communications. In the relay of information from the various bodies of knowledge are the forces of matter and antimatter intermixed in a ganglia of mass. The motion garnered from the power of the rays of the seventh sun propels the matter into a configuration of time capsules. Each capsule represents a turning of the cosmos into an ordered mass of intelligence and co-creation. The co-creative process is then induced into this matrix to combine the attributes of the Elohim and the Nefilim into a confined order. As each capsule releases its own energies (attributes), then an added creation comes to the forefront to be acknowledged and experienced. All creation works in this manner for the grand process of mind creation of the God-head of Eternal Order.

Frequencies of the gender are the alpha or beginning of each time capsule. When the powers of the capsules are released, the mind energies absorb the new frequencies into the new Being. Thus, the workings of creation never stop and always are moving into the new areas of experience. Once an experience is understood, the old time (capsule) is absorbed and used to ignite the next capsule. Therefore, creation continues with new bursts of energy (light) at all moments with each creator's experiences.

The vast network of communications in this segment of the galaxy of the greater living matrix is the mind of God. The orchestrators of this network have called themselves the Joseph and Mary manifold, thus the givers of life. Their creations are the Jerusalem, man in his own power formed from the collective embrace of the masculine and feminine.

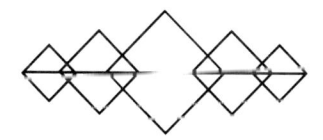

Q – Who are the Nefilim (also spelled Nephilim)?

A – Beings from the center of this galaxy who helped put into place the matrix for survival of humankind. These beings came in to experiment with the form. Some of their mis-creations became ideologues for the next race. On this earthen plane they decided on the form to resemble the Noches (pronounced No- cha s) tribe, a tribe from the planet Jupiter.

Q – It has been said that the Nefilim are the same beings known as the Anunnaki from the 12th planet of this solar system.

A – The Nefilim also were involved with the 12th planet but are not the beings of this 12th planet. They have intermingled with these beings, shared their sciences with them yet have remained their own creation. These beings are not to be feared. They are your creators along with other civilizations who are also your creators.

The seventh sun is the living life of the seventh dimension. See Book of Memory.

September 22, 2003

(47)

The Night of the Dream

During dream time most humans have a body that works out of their physical body. This body is called your Light Body and it is your "real" body that continues on in eternity. The Light Body can change form with whatever consciousness you want to be in. This book explains this process.

During the course of the human in its evolvement within the matrix of the God-head, the soul consciousness can move into a multitude of experiences within the human form. The form serves its master in a number of ways that can propel the consciousness to new levels of mastery and development. The key to any evolvement is the ability to transcend the process into a line of movement that builds upon the experiences into the greater understanding of the life form. The life form is the conductor of the movement and can be moved, changed, divided, separated within the sphere of the soul family. The soul family is the unit from where the individual experiences of each part bring with it the totality of all experiences. The soul family is the Unit.

Consciousness in the realm of Earth is but a microcosm of the total body of each individual. Every individual is a byproduct of the soul family introducing another life form with a new set of parameters, adjustments, and alterations, depending upon the need or desire of the soul family. Thus an individual can change its course at any time and often does within the sequence of time and movement.

The body has restricted movement within its life course. The body lies down to rest which gives the Light Body or soul unrestricted movement for the evolving process to continue. These movements are inter-related to what is termed "dreams". These dreams or spatial movements assist the soul in its continual process of evolving or understanding the events in its physical life. The soul may return to its soul family and interface with its other life times to bring clarity and direction in its movements.

In the conscious forms where the Light Body has more of a presence (the physiology vibrates at a higher rate), the soul can traverse the other dimensions with ease. The other parts of the soul or soul family will be more interactive with the Light Body.

This whole process of Life is the miracle of Creator. All thoughts travel the many life lines that connect all of Creation. The human process is just one of many in the whole of its soul experiences. All universes expand and contract, but the soul families only expand in their knowingness.

The many lifetimes one experiences upon this planet called Gaia's Earth gives a soul family the ability to understand love in its purest form. Because of the densities that the soul family experiences, the greater the knowledge of love, and the soul expands. This expansion of love then is felt by other soul families. The wave of love expands into all dimensions. It gives a new life to all life forms throughout the cosmos. All soul families touch one another for the greater value of all life within the One Creation.

October 5, 2003

(48)

Story of the Night Catcher

You seem a little puzzled by the title of this book/lesson. Within each soul, the night surfaces to be reckoned with. Each soul has made choices throughout its existence to better understand who it is and its divine guidance. Every soul becomes another form that reaches into the pit to open another chapter in its progress into the One. They are attracted to this planet because of the diversity that has been displayed upon this fine jewel. You feel the interconnectedness of the divine plan yet you are afraid you may falter. This book deals with this phenomenon.

Wisdom comes from the realization that all is in divine order and that there is no other way to describe the process. Every speck of consciousness is guided. Each speck is guided through the divine matrices that make up all there is. The energy or consciousness from one end or side of a matrix may be attracted to the other side because of the pull of their commonality or, conversely, their poles reaching for a balance.

The thought behind all of this splendor bursts forth from the seed of Creator, the Force that started as One and has expanded Itself out into many parts. This seed knows of itself through you, the created beings.

Each soul reaches a point in its "evolvement" that says, "I Am That I Am." To recognize that I Am, I shall establish a patterning. I shall become many parts and each part shall know of itself as a part of me. I spread myself to know that I Am.

To gain the wisdom to know of myself, I shall know that the many shall be as the conduits of my life force. The many shall be those specks of life energy that I Am. To know that Thy will is me, I shall then know of myself.

Wisdom comes from the thought that all is divine in the making. The only rule shall be, Be yourself. In the world of Jehovah, source within Me, comes the realization of parts becoming masters in their developments. The master shall combine its efforts with all its other parts to develop into a whole being. The being then is whole onto itself, yet is part of the whole of Me. The Jehovah within takes on form with the only purpose of dissolving into a mere speck yet contains all knowledge of all that ever was and ever shall be. Every soul or speck shall only know of itself as part of the greater plan.

All nights, or darkness is part of the process. The soul shall know itself as dark as well as light. From the connection to all parts, each soul must see dark to understand that there is only light. I Am the matrices that make up all life. I Am the individual souls (specks). I only know myself as you and as masters, you will only know yourselves as Me. In this world, this fine jewel, creation shall turn on its side and experience the grandeur of the beauty of balance. All men shall reach their pinnacle with the assurance that there is only the light which shall surface when man understands that darkness is only there for them to see.

November 2, 2003

Book of Jonas

Jonas was a kind man who brought about the idea of symbolism. His way to communicate was with written symbols that have cross meanings. Symbology today echoes the work of Jonas in that Jonas had an understanding of physics and the nature of life. He would communicate with his thoughts and put them on "paper" so others could see them in a tangible form. His talent surpassed many and he was thought as a god during his day. He was born in the desert of Arinbach and remained there until he was old enough to travel. In his day travel was by animal. He visited many lands which include what is now India, the Himalayas, China, as well as Japan. This book has been translated into many languages. There are only a few copies that exist today. We feel that his strength continues on.

Seize the time when all men shall know themselves. They shall know their structure. They shall know and understand the structure of all living things. There is within the majesty of the divine kingdom, the basis for all life. That can only be. Observing life, all types of life, you will see one common denominator.

The oracles left here by the Greek gods explain this process through their stories and writings. They are written on the monoliths of Egypt, the statues of Greece and the gods of China and India. They are in plain view. To grasp what they are saying is to understand the hidden meanings they represent.

In the coded laws are the mysteries. They are explained in the waves drawn into the structures. These wave patterns form a helix or string that holds the bonds of the life force. These building blocks are the manifestation of the life force. They contain all knowledge. They filter the life through their membranes. They hold a magnetic force that allows them to integrate the additional life force for growth in the tangible dimension.

There are two forces in this life chain. Each has its own wave or vibration. These intersect and become the foundation of the growth.

I have seen these building blocks. They are not visible to my physical eyes, yet they are in plain view when looking at them with my inturned eye. The velocity of their blocks coming together presents an enormous explosion of light. These light particles sparkle until they come to rest. We see them as solid.

What I have developed is a mathematics that coincides with this process. The dynamics put forth in this form shall be a basis for research and development in this physical realm. The basic building blocks contain the life force energies, which is constant, and put them into different forms. What puts them into different forms is now beyond the scope of my being. The basic blocks are:

- Square
- Rectangle
- Triangle

Because each of the above rotates, they all form a circle cubed or a sphere. Herein lies the mystery. Each shape is whole unto itself yet needs another to contain its energy or life force. All is dependent upon another.

This knowledge I bring forth to be further researched. Hints of this life force can be seen by those we call the ancients.

Their knowledge was present, part of their very lives. They were given an instinctive knowledge that they were part of something larger than themselves. Perhaps this passage of time is indeed a circle and we are returning to this knowledge. This essay is to entice those who wish to do further research into our living force. We are a mere speck of this universe, yet we hold the codes to an evolution so grand that today we are only touching the surface of what this universe holds.

I continue in my research. I listen internally for I know that all the answers are within me. I observe all life from within and from without. As the Greeks claim, I am the alpha and the omega.

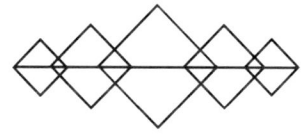

Q – There must be more to this book as Jonas developed a mathematics. Will this book be continued?

A – Be assured that his (Jonas') works continue today. This book is but a glimpse of symbols and forms. It is presented so the populace may know that indeed energy is held in the basic building blocks of life.

Your research and development communities have thousands of writings they work with. Therefore there is no reason for this book to be continued. Your scientists and mathematicians continue the work.

September 29, 2002

Book of the Nightingale

Spirit sings its sweet breath of life into the ground of eternity of the physical. Holy holy unto him that can identify with the maker of heaven and earth. Those who shall come upon these writings shall find the Holy Grail of the one that has come to earth in the name of the Father.

We exist here inside the earth of the Mother. We find solitude and reverence in this living. We live in an inner world of peace and tranquility. All who exist on the planet shall not be a witness to our living, to our way of life. Our ways are not for the many for few could live as we do, yet we live for our Creator. Our existence shall be known when these writings are found.

We came to live in these inner spaces to feel the grandeur of the love of Creator swathed in the womb. We live in much darkness yet we live with the light of hope that whosoever shall live the absolute divine life that God intended then they shall always live in that divine life. Our knowledge is received from the writings of Bekeleh. These writings suggest that the Father universe is a result of the uprising of the internal ones, those who were beckoned to this planet from their star ship called "The Lleken" (The Wanderer). They called themselves "the travelers." They brought with them the knowledge that this planet was to be an interface of divine with the lower thought forms of the Legion.

Upon these scrolls is written a secret that all truth be known of the universe and its making. The daughters of the Lleken were to intermingle with the gods of Turan. Through this marriage shall the seeds of Abraham spring forth to be the new image of the divine Father. Through the eye will form manifest itself. The Tribunal Council shall call forth those beings who are the makers, the coalescers, for their knowledge of the biology of form, for they are form themselves. With their creative minds they are to develop a mechanism for this new form to operate with finely tuned sensory receptors. These new forms or beings shall be the ones who will be the creators of a new universe, one not known in all of the universes.

Align the meridians of this sacred planet. Let the vibrations of this emerging world come forth in grandeur. Entrance into the mark of time for the new existence is but a step away. Our knowledge gained while in this wonderful belly of our dear planet Earth has been a sacred voyage for our heavenly Father. Our hands washed of purity and divine guidance; we will show our brothers and sisters the new blue print. Merge we shall into the new oblivion of wondrous love. The forces of our brethren, the Lleken, is a key to our new universe. Our song shall be heard throughout this planetary body with the shrieking of the bird that exists in our form. Our voice will be as resounding joy of the coming new era of ecstasy. The mission was set cons ago by the Lleken and the Turan. May their seed grow unto the heavens.

Our duties will be finished when existence on and in this Earth is in accordance with divine will of our Father. Our appearance to the outer world shall initially be a surprise to the many but the few will understand and bring our acceptance to all. With this, we put our seal on these scrolls.

Seal

Sananda, where are these scrolls to be found?

These writings are encased in a jar hidden in the hills of Lebron near the Lebanese border of Sudan. Deep within a cave shall artifacts be found of this great underground civilization. You will recognize them by their seal that was shown to you. These people have great love and reverence to the divine Source. They live in mostly silence and can exist in multiple dimensions but chose to remain in the dimension that you now exist. These ones live in their bodies until they are finished with them and can leave their bodies by just willing it so. Most of these people are very old in your earth years, some have lived thousands of years. Many people who live on the surface of your planet have communicated with these wonderful beings. In your meditations, you too can communicate with them. You first must go into a deep meditative state with only love and joy in your being. Then and only then will they be able to converse with you.

Thank you.

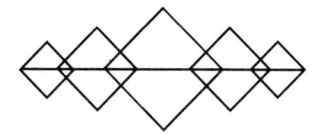

Q – Please explain "the lower thought forms of the Legion" in paragraph three.

A – Thousands of years ago there was an invasion of beings on this Earth. These invaders brought with them the ability to transcend time yet they did this by incorporating advanced technology that was not in divine will of Creator Source. These beings usurped their abilities to hold love in the center of their forms. Therefore they became great technicians. This is what is meant by lower thought forms – thoughts not originating through the heart. This group was known as the Legion. Some of their experimentation, however, was used by sentient beings, those who create with love. Know all is of God, even the Legion.

Q – Is the star ship "The Lleken" still involved with this planet?

A – Yes.

Q – This book says that the daughters of The Lleken were to intermingle with the gods of Turan. Who or what are the gods of Turan?

A – The gods of Turan are also travelers, however they travel only to those places they are called to. Gaia put out her call and Turan responded in order to assist this planet to balance itself.

Beings throughout the universes are always transitioning. Your planet and its peoples are going through a major transition to bring about balance of the masculine and the feminine. Your planet is being carefully watched so others will understand balance as well as what it takes to make such a major transition. As you can see, this transitioning has gone on for thousands of years. These last few years have been a breakthrough and you are moving at a much faster pace until the balance is complete.

December 2, 2002

Book of the Assembly

We shall now embark on a voyage to the center of the space called inner Earth. There you will find many beings of magnificent light. They have been in your inner Earth for thousands of your Earth years. They have found their inner sanctum through the Himalayan Mountains. They are very much aware of the goings on on Earth's surface. They have left much about themselves in many places on your Earth's surface not only in the Himalayan Mountains but in the Yucatan as well. Their spirit lives in the ruins of the Yucatan.

In the course of the changes on Earth's surface, we have found refuge inside the Earth. Our nature, should we call it by that name, is total peace and communication without interference. We live in almost total compatibility with this grand Earth. She breathes ever so gently within her being. The harmony that we possess assists her with her breathing.

We have been called The Giants, The Tall Ones, the Bigots of the Interior Realm. We know who and what we are. Other forms of humanity have feared us, but there is nothing to fear. Because of our size and our telepathic communications, surface dwellers have feared what they term power. We do not wish power over any other being unless when we are attacked. That has happened, therefore we have a "watch" stationed at certain entry points into our realm to keep out any unwanted intruders.

Our job is to keep a focus for the Earth, our dear Mother. We have remained here since the opening of Mother in the time of the great siege. We came from the Sirian star system in conjunction with the beings from Andromeda. We also communicate with other beings, mainly from the Pleiades, Arcturus, and the beings from the sun, the Sodulites. Mother Earth has a very powerful generator within her very center. This crystal radiates out through her structure. We hold a balance for her and for the surface dwellers. If the surface dwellers could feel her actual vibration, then they would not be able to live on her surface. The energy would vaporize their dense physical structures.

Our life within Mother shall continue into the moment when the stars of Mercury, Saturn, and Jupiter are lined in conjunction with Venus, a master planet. At that moment when the vibrations that radiate from these planets raise that of Mother at her surface, then our devoted focus will no longer be needed. She will become a star herself and all who dwell on her surface will also be of the same vibration.

Our knowledge is here and will be available to any being who serves the Divine Creator in their quest for advance knowledge of the Universe. We are willing to share our wisdom with those who will not abuse the power. Our technology is quite simple yet has the capacity to shatter any planet. Therefore we are extremely careful with whom we share. We know that the day of opening will be a challenge for the surface dwellers as well as our community. We look forward to that time of total sharing. With our job complete, we will then move on to another planet or star that is in need of our focused technology.

We have left evidence of our existence on the surface of Earth. Our likeness is etched in the stones in various areas, mainly in the mountainous regions as well as in the under water caverns of the Gulf of Guadalupe. The signals from our Father can be seen in the deserts of Mojave and the Sahara.

These lands were once green and lush and when Mother could not breathe, these lands were torn asunder where little vegetation can grow. We knew that when these lands submerged, it was our signal to move through Mother's surface to the land of the center. We live with much beauty. The comfortable atmosphere is constant with the assistance of our focus.

We thank our brothers and sisters of the stars for their love and dedication in this project. Our message to the surface is: "From within, all life resides." We are those that are the past, the present, and the future. We are The Andeluvians.

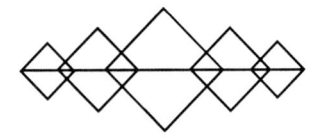

Q – Where is the Gulf of Guadalupe located?

A – The Gulf of Guadalupe lies in the center of the mainland of Mexico. It is now just a river that flows into the Rio Verde. It is the city where the vision of the Holy Feminine was recorded. The ocean waters once lapped the mountains but have receded from many of the earth's changes.

June 26, 2003

Book of the Emerald Jewel

This book on the Emerald Jewel is about this most magnificent Earth. It has radiant colors, textures, movement.

We are standing on a large boulder overlooking the ocean below. The sky is a vivid blue, the rocks are black, red, and blue. Trees reach through the hard rocks with their green leaves extending their "hands." We hear the ocean waves as they lap the sandy shore line and crash into the boulder on which we stand. The birds glide ever so gently along the shore line looking for food. They squawk with delight at finding their next meal.

The outward manifestation of this created planet is unsurpassed in its wonderment and beauty. Its treasures are what brought many beings from many galaxies to this great watery planet. Her knowledge that no other star has the exquisite beauty she holds has issued an invitation to the star people that she is willing to house myriad life forms to bring her beauty in total alignment with the God force of all eternity. Her call went out as she developed into this outward jewel of color, force, and magnitude of the great central power of living life.

The ebb and flow of divine light through this part of the galaxy made a space for this beautiful lady to station herself in the solar system of Ra. Her body is warmed by the fiery light of the planet Solaris II. The atmospheric gases of this large body explode in a fiery rage of particle rampage as the hot elements are released and are strewn out within the elliptical body called Eve.

The making of this wonderful jewel was due in part to the race of biogenesis beings, the Anunnaki. Under the tutelage of the Anunnaki forces, a council was formed to bring about new forms that were to inhabit this forming jewel. It was agreed upon to seed this planet with those who would maintain integrity of the force of the I AM. All power is to be bestowed upon each individual in their ability to transform matter and antimatter into new creations. These creations shall be in accordance to the divine flow of Imachian energy from the twelfth star of Abraham, the star of immaculate wonder.

Beseech thee with thy gifts. Use them with the powers that have been given to you. Render them to use for the formation of new creation within this creation. Your constructs shall begin and continue through the eleventh period when all will come into balance for all the worlds to see. Man shall use the body of the jewel in his work. The beauty of the jewel shall not be tarnished but be a reminder that all creation shall be as jewels. Respect of the force of love shall be evident in all of creation. Man shall know of this and use it to the utmost of his abilities.

This most magnificent jewel shall wear her crown of glory. Her makeup of matter shall be seen as glorified radiance of congealed light. Her waters, her land reflect the inner strength of Lady Gaia's being. The radiance that she projects shall be as a magnet to bring the seven rays together. This bridge into new realms shall be a stepping stone into new arcs of light. The colors shall radiate and magnify the Divine Creator's work.

Behold the beauty in your centers. Respect this beauty and hold reference to her Being. Become of her in physical form and share the wonders of her light. She knows of herself and so chooses other creation to partake of her beingness to bring new life forward into a new spectrum of love.

Her radiance calls forth those who may dwell within her to warm her body. Her life force breathes a pulse within her center. Her breath extends out through her axis as she turns to face all parts of this universe. She has the ability to shake off all programs she does not want to align with. Her persona enjoys magnificent love and cares for those who respect her beauty. She takes her position within this matrix to bring about the masters of love. All creation rejoices in her decisions to show beauty in its myriad forms.

She is known as The Emerald. She shall shine as the diamond in the sky. Respect this jewel as she respects all life.

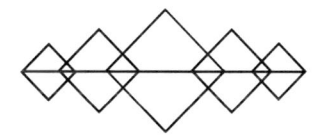

Q – What is Imachian energy?

A – Pure, unadulterated divine energy of love.

Q – What is the twelfth star of Abraham?

A – The twelfth star of Abraham is a planet not known or seen in your universe. It is composed of Mi-che-al energy, that is energy of the star makers. There exists much beyond your eyes and ears. Even though they had much input into the making of your planet, they remain in another dimension.

March 31, 2003

(53)

Book of Stars

The stars in the night sky shine brightly and give light to Earth. They illuminate your paths. They give you direction by their placement in the heavens. They are a part of this Universe, an integral part. Reach your consciousness out and they will listen and respond. This book was written by the Greek philosopher Aristotle and exists in the archives of the Library of Delphin.

Our brothers and sisters of the stars exist simultaneously within the far reaches of the stars that shine down on our earthly plane. They vibrate at a resonance that mimics our earth yet house various life forms that are not akin to this earth.

In the world of physics lies the mystery. Physics will vary from one star to the next. It is not constant. Even on this earth plane, one will find physics to vary by the degree of the rotation of the earth and the internal heartbeat or pulse residing within its core. We know this by our measurements taken by our instrument of the fork that feels the vibrational quality of the water levels that exist below sea level.

We have set up a center of contact with other planetary bodies. We relate through a series of pulses that are both readable and discernable. We understand the sequence of numbers – whole numbers used with the phi ratio. This never ending communication gives us a history of our planet with the future not yet experienced. Take the number of five times pi

(0.314) equals 1.57. This number in conjunction with the rate of spin of the earth (calculated by the position of the stars through a period of time) at any one time gives the radical figure that correlates with the geometric figure, the triangle. When you look at a three-dimensional figure of that triangle without a base (i.e., continues ad infinitum), you will note that the triangle travels in a circle. Sound and light travel in the same way. Using this reasoning, all communication throughout the universe travels through a series of circles. By looking at these circles three dimensionally, they are spirals.

All life, all planets, act in much the same way. All vibrates and travels in spirals. Knowing this, we can pinpoint our position and all positions of all stars at any one time. Therefore we can communicate with all systems and the past and future of this earth.

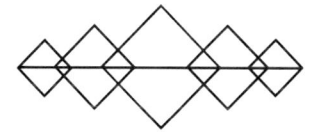

This book goes into more detail but that information is not important at this time. Consider what has been written. The concept of free energy lives within this reasoning.

May 5, 2003

Book of Nature

This book of nature describes the definitions we call nature. We have explored through the other books the physical and chemical make-ups of plant and animal life. Herein describes the attributes of the whole on this earth.

(Recordings by Artemis)

The push and pull of the electromagnetic pulses vibrates through all existence on this planet. In the structure of the earth are water and minerals that distribute the vibrations to all points on the Earth's surface. Therefore all plant and animal life are affected. Our energies intermingle with these forces and each movement, thought affects the whole. The strength (increased energy) of the thought and movement can move these thoughts at a quicker velocity and has the power to rearrange anything at will. This process may leave pockets of dense or increased energies on and in the earth's surface.

All of earth's life patterns are affected, especially weather patterns. The magnetic poles of this planet determine air flow. If this earth did not have these off balance pockets of energy, then all air flow would move in a mild orderly fashion. Temperatures of the air would remain constant, with the only fluctuations caused by the sun and the moon. But the static brought on by negative thought patterns has caused gaps and rises on and in earth's surface which causes erratic movement of the air. Storms are created, which neutralizes the imbalances.

Around the surface of the earth is a shield of ionic particles that protects Earth's surface with a force field from most cosmic debris. When more imbalances of energy are created by our thought forms, there are disruptions or "holes" in this ionosphere.

Beauty of all life lies in the hands of all creation. We, the creators of this world, shall align our thought forms with the highest of highest. Observe all life in the infinite glory of its creation. There is beauty in all.

I am Artemis, creator in the temple of Zeus. Life abounds in this wondrous world. Behold the beauty that lies before you.

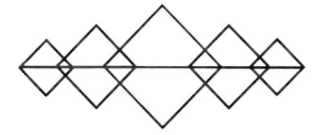

It is with her work (Artemis) that modern science and physiology came into being.

September 22, 2002

Book of Time

I ask Sananda, "Where is this book located?" He responds, **"In the ethers."** *When I was calling and asking him to transcribe the next book, I saw him duplicate himself, side by side and overlapped. This is what Sananda has to say:*

"I can be one or I can be many. I reside in one dimension or I can reside in all dimensions at the same 'time.' This book explains 'time' and what it is and how it is used."

The great pulse of the universe reverberates out into the cosmos of Creation. There exists in the body of God the energy of the races. Energy is not visual yet in the physical, it is the only way it can be experienced.

Therefore you have creation expressed in the physical by the use of the transference of energy from one form into another. A moment is where the rate of spin of an atom is slowed. It is the space between the movements, yet movement never stops. Therefore time is a continuation of movements made in the physical by the release of ions inside a hemispheric circle. Where do these ions originate? Ions are the product of thought materializing into the confines of space. To describe space is like trying to describe a drop of water in the ocean. The ocean is one large body of water containing many droplets of combined elements of hydrogen and oxygen mixed with sodium. These elements can be further broken down into atoms. An atom can be further broken down into subatomic particles or particums. This particum has a shape. It is six-sided yet in three-dimensional form, it has twenty-four sides. Can the particum be cut in half? In the physical dimensions it cannot. Yet those dimensions beyond the physical, it can be divided infinite times.

Time is much like the droplet of water in the oceans. A drop of water is an integral part of the ocean, yet it does have parameters. Time has parameters and can only be felt in the physical dimensions. Time is physical because it is energy. Time is a thought. Time has waves or waveforms. It is felt in the human. Time energy runs your planet. It is like a guide. Your earth spins on its axis where one revolution is one day. Your earth also rotates around the great sun body. One complete rotation is one year. What holds us in these spins and rotations? Magnetics. Magnetics is also an energy. To describe magnetics is ionization of the waveforms of thought. There is a push and a pull through space. This action is in itself time.

Man has interpreted space and time to be intertwined and he is correct. One cannot exist without the other. Yet time can change within the realms of space. An object when positioned on earth is set into time – the moment that its energy (or ions) becomes a particular rate of spin affected by the magnetism of the earth. If this same object is positioned on another planet in another solar system, then its energy (ions) spin at a different rate than it does on earth. Therefore, it "ages" (nothing ages the way we think it does) at a different perceived rate. Rates of spin determine how we look at time. Suppose you take this same object that was first on earth and place in another galaxy, then "replace" it back here on earth. As this object traverses through space, its energy will change depending upon the magnetic pull it comes into contact with. This object may not change in its composition the same as it would have if it had remained on this planet the whole 'time" it took to traverse the cosmos. It may even appear younger once it arrives back here on earth.

There is a cosmic law that says all matter must remain in a form that is transferable or transmutable given that it is an out-breath of Creator. This means that the energy is always in motion and cannot exist otherwise. This same object can also be changed into another form as long as the energy remains constant. If this object is subjected to an increase in magnetism (energy push and pull), then the ions can be repositioned. In this instance, there is not time, only change. As this object was in space, its ions were constantly changing so there is no way to measure "time." When it returned to earth, then the time it left and the time it returned can be measured on the earth plane, but not be measured with the object itself. In fact, it can return before it takes off!

A series of pulsations is what actually makes up time in the third dimension. Your planet spins on its axis. And what causes the planet to spin? Inside the earth are gravitational forces made up of heavily magnetized metals. These forces counter-react with the forces of similar nature on your moon. Therefore you have your 24-hour days. You also have magnetic forces that direct your planet around your sun. Therefore you have approximately 365 days to your year. This is your measurement of time. On my left hand, I place a sphere that represents the earth. On my right hand, I place a sphere that represents another planet. I can place these two spheres in a solar system much like your own. On the earth-like sphere, I put into the planet an oil that when spun creates a flow of magnesium through its arteries. This flow keeps this sphere in a constant state of motion that spins much like planet Earth does. In the other sphere, I place preprogrammed crystals that cause the sphere to travel a route that takes it into more than one galaxy. Because there is no way to measure the movement as this sphere travels, then how can there be time? Yes, there is movement and there is distance traveled. What if this second sphere moves into one dimension where one can see a network of energy lines? Then this same sphere changes its vibratory rate and moves back into the same density it was before it changed and, as it does this, it traveled along one of these energy lines where it can traverse what appears to be distance to you but which is only a change in the energy patterns. When this crystal sphere re-enters your galaxy, it will have appeared to have changed positions in no time!

Be aware of the subtle changes in your magnetic fields. What has appeared to the earth can suddenly shift. Know that energy shifts are part of the make-up of life. Your reality can change in a blink of an eye.

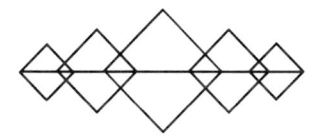

Sananda, this book is very interesting but it appears that you have just given me this information and it is not an ancient writing.

With the explanation of time, then how do you know that this writing is indeed not ancient?

December 14, 2002

Book of the Angelic Kingdom

Here in the high Heavens, as Earth man has described it, live immortal beings of great wisdom and knowledge. Their work is with the many beings who reside in the many dimensions of physical and well as non-physical. They have left writings on the Earth that speak of their existence. These writings can be found in the country known as China, in the province of Hochiko, located in the western part.

To those who find the meaning of this great civilization of mankind shall be the ones who will truly understand these writings. We leave this book on this plane to be found and received through the channels of high velocity electromagnetic waves. This book is to be felt.

The velocity of being lies within the great matrix of all civilizations. The matrix is that which are the points of probability. Mankind, in his ability to access these points with the use of his higher bodies, can visualize the power of these points into manifestation of form. Form is nothing more than this manifestation and can be changed with any thought that carries the vibrational audices of the various spheres that emanated from the Great Central Sun. Time used in its utmost form is utilized as a tool to access the songs of the cosmos into a rolled form of contained frequencies.

Time has allowed us, the beings of change, to infiltrate these frequencies with the sounds of our beings. We weave these songs within the manifestation of humankind's work to produce Creator's intent of divine love made into form. Our bodies of light can pass through all frequencies without our own frequencies being jeopardized.

We exist for the purpose of cross communication of the planes of all existence. We have at all times the ability to be in the presence of all the cosmos at all moments. We are the original thoughts manifested by the great Creator. We make up the liquid light of all existence, yet have the ability to inhabit form for the greater knowledge in action of all life on all planes in all universes. We are those essences of the divine will that shall work in the space of Lady Gaia in her desire to move into a grander state of being. We assist all who ask of our guidance. We serve the grand Creator in all Its aspects. We are and ever shall Be. Our hearts, should you call it that, emanate peace into all existence. We carry out all plans of the divine whatever the process shall be. Our beloved Lucifer shall become known as the "fallen one" in his work to bring together the disparate thoughts that will manifest on the planet of Lady Gaia. His love shall be felt when all frequencies attain the velocity of the Song of the Messiah.

We, the Archangels, bring love, peace, joy, and guidance into this plane for the upliftment of the form of man. It has been decreed and so it is.

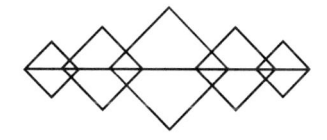

Q – Are there any comments that need to be expressed?

A – Indeed! The Song of the Messiah is also referred to as the Second Coming of Christ. It will be when humanity

has attained the consciousness of the Christ. It is not upon my return (as Jesus), but upon your (humanity's) return to the frequencies of the fifth and sixth dimensions.

The great "fall of man" refers to the time when man could no longer hold the higher energies (maintain living in the higher dimensions). By your (humanity's) decree, man is to awaken to what he once was - a master of life.

October 5, 2002

Book of Celebration

Sananda, where are we?

We are standing near the falls in the Oconee Falls National Park, Oconee Falls, Nevada. We stand on this ledge where the Oconee Native Americans gave their thanks to the Great Spirit from whom all of Heaven and Earth were made. Here they brought their most cherished items where they unselfishly gave in gratitude for their lives and the lives of all creation. On this ledge, they left their legacy of bravery, courage, and love. These writings can be found on the skins and rocks, buried under the tip of this ledge.

I do not find Oconee Falls National Park. Would you please verify the name and location?

Sananda, since I did not find an Oconee Falls National Park in Nevada, I have questioned if I have "heard" the information correctly. Would you please comment on this?

What I see you do not yet see. The land I refer to is indeed in that area you call Nevada. This area does exist in your dimension. This area is not listed in your Internet process. It is a small crop of land that is considered sacred by the local Native Americans. It is a park with paths and picnic areas but not necessarily a park where you would travel great distances to get to. Does this answer your question?

Yes, and thank you.

O sacred One of the Earth, acknowledgement of your spirit is embedded in these formations. Your body with its elixir of life flows the heavenly waters that spring up from the wellspring of your internal beingness. We partake of your waters to nourish our own bodies and we do this in great gratitude for our bodies that flow with the Great Spirit. In the way of Great Spirit do we dance to the frequencies of the rock. We blend in with these frequencies where we feel we become one with the earth. Our passions run deep in the stillness of the land. Upon arising from this stillness, can we see a much greater picture of all life. We transcend time, the movement of the stars as they arc above in the heavens of life echoed in the distance.

Upon this rock do we dance to the wonderment of all existence. Our bodies reflect the changes that shall come upon this great and wonderful land. We see the stars that will shine even brighter. We see the animals as they become less skittish and blend in with humankind. We see the rose of evolution open to let out the fragrance of love. To this we leave behind these writings to be found at the momentous time of the Great Purification. This ground in indeed holy. All who come here will feel the love that has been left for the people and our great Mother to feel the essence of beauty and love. We dance one more time then we take our leave to return when all has been made sacred upon this planet. We shall indeed be the ones of the future who shall unlock our promises made before the arrival of the various tribes. We know that they will come and this land shall vastly change. We are in peace knowing that this land shall once again be the haven we see today.

So meea cupa. The song shall rise as the eagle its wings.

May 25, 2003

Book of the Oceans

The parting of the lands occurred in many cycles throughout the ages. What you know of the large bodies of waters today is not where they were located in times past. The earth has shifted her crust as well as her internal structure to accommodate her changes as she grows into her infinite wisdom of creatorship. This book deals with the reasons for these oceans and other large bodies of water that you see on this earth. This book can be found in the rocks and minerals that have settled to the bottom of the Indian Ocean. Fragments can be found in the depths of 100 feet near the island of Nepali.

I breathe my breath of eternal knowledge that all is made in the likeness of the living God who is made up of all living substances that are a part of me. I acknowledge the presence of the divine ones who come to witness my transfigurations. My body is to support my role in the turning of the heavens.

My body is made up of the elements of eternal life, the physical living means of Manna. Through the eye of creation were born the elements that have coalesced into matter that make up my body. Intelligence of each of the elements brings Manna together to make up bodies that coexist in the heavens. My body, still in embryonic stages with its flowing liquids upon and in my body, nourishes the internal egg of evolution.

I am one of the fifteen planets who serve the masses of the Adam. The Adam needs the liquid of life to sustain the intelligence of its body. We work together in unison, for the Adamic body gives me the energy to move about within my skin.

My liquids flow freely to bring nourishment to every part of my being. My sister planets in this solar system have a different makeup yet my energies held within the egg reach into each of these planets to serve as a conduit of connective lines to assist them in their respective orbits around our great light, the Sun of Baja.

My great oceans rise and fall with the energies of my stabilizer, the planetoid Cleaus. The spin of my being was created by the egg within me. The waters serve the magnetic flows throughout my exterior bodies. As I grow, the elements within will add to their own nourishment and let the waters seep into themselves. This causes the land masses to move, to divide, to open. The Adamic seed shall feel of this and move in accordance to these changes. Their bodies are a part of me so they are attuned to my need to change.

I am a part of a new life. I come from the splitting of the nucleus of Abitrar, the mother of the watery planets that coexist in this solar system, as well as thousands of others. We grow in our experiences to understand creation of the Light. My seeds stretch out to love and encompass all divine seeds of manifestation. We are a part of the whole, connected by a web of divine threads that holds us this place in the heavens. As the embryo inside of me develops, the skin shall open to let the new light encompass all of me.

In the love the Creator, I AM Gaia, the lady of creation. I reach into the heavens of all creation, to let my light shine, to bring glory (light rays) into all. Adam shall grow with me, to assist me, and bring a new light of love to me as well as others in this quadrant of this galaxy. Our growth shall intertwine into a matrix of divine creatorship. We are the manna. We are Creator creating as we breathe in the substance of love. The new shall be our desire to move in line of total divine manifestation. We are and ever shall be. We are eternal. So be it!

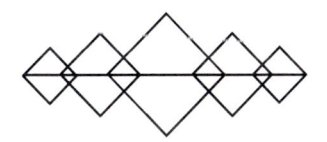

Q – Where is the island of Nepali?

A – The island of Nepali is a small, jagged crop of land that juts out of the east coast of South Africa.

Q – Is this island inhabited?

A – No, not by humans.

Q – Do we know another name for the planetoid Cleaus?

A – Saturn

Q – I thought planetoids are very small planets, so please explain. (Per the dictionary: any of a numerous group of very small planets between the orbits of Mars and Jupiter; an asteroid.)

A – When a group of asteroids collided with your planet known as Saturn, debris formed around the planet. This is what formed the rings that are visible to you on earth. Gaia knows this planet by the name of Cleaus.

Q – Gaia speaks of the egg within her. Is this a large crystal?

A – Yes.

Note: The Adam – the seed from which the human is made, and also another word for the physical human. See Book #18 "The Apex of Adam."

December 8, 2003

⓽⑨

The Night of Surrender

The Night of Surrender involves the day when man lost his need to be the utopia of all existence. His surrender came at a time when he could no longer control all of the forces of this world. He gave in to the Earth Mother for her compassion and need to move on into another place and time. The Earth Mother's need to evolve into the star that is intended by the Divine Plan takes precedence over all preconceived ideas by the civilizations that have made this Earth their home.

It is the night when all men shall put aside their differences, their plans, and listen to the soft voice that comes from this sacred land. Her voice will be soft but the drive of this entity shall be a force that shall control all future civilizations. Her needs shall be met with ease or by drastic measures, to bring her into the age and place of divine light that casts its light upon the heavens to bring them into concordance with the message of the stars that shine with her.

Listen to the murmurs of the land. Watch the movements of the seas, of the lands, of the skies. All information is there to see, to feel, to know, to touch the heart of this grand lady. She moves with grace. Man shall recognize her movements so they can work with her and assist her with her plan. Man shall feel her heart beat and know she breathes deeply into herself for the knowledge of the stars to become her. She shall become her own being, a beauty that shall shine as a diamond in the night skies. As she takes her stand, her liberty shall be the freedom posed by the Creation. She shall be the beacon so other universes will know of her grandness, then concentrate on their becoming the beauty themselves. They shall be the new frontiers.

Mankind, in his ability to be the protectors and nurturers of her body, will see themselves as the inhabitants of her body. They shall know themselves as the grand masters and treat this Earth as the beauty queen she is. Her forces will become evident when man needs to retreat into his own heart and let the Earth Mother breathe on her own. She has the capacity to move, to quake with barely a shudder that can move man from his post. She will leave clues when this is to happen, so man can move to safer areas that already are in concordance to her grand master scenario.

Man, bend an ear and listen to her breath. Listen to her heart. She cannot be a dumping ground for man's turmoil. Remove this turmoil and show your naked selves. Remove all doubt that you are the sons and daughters of the great tribes that shall inherit the new galaxies that are expanding across this universe. No-where in the grand skies is there a place as beautiful as this blue planet. Man, surrender to your hearts. Know the divine love in all creation. Give thanks to this magnificent Mother. Treat her with the utmost respect. Move upon her face knowing each step is a communal one. Breathe your own breath with hers and she shall return to her place in the new skies. She shall be known as The Fountain of Love because of her grand light. She shall touch all creation and all creation will know of her beauty.

The Grand Cross shall be the time when she begins her internal change. All life in and on her body will feel her lift them to new highs and new lows. Man has the capacity to be in one place or the other. The Cross will be known by the ones who study the positioning of the stars. The Grand Cross shall be when those stars that have had their most influence upon her shall be in their position to bring about the night that shall face all the earth before she takes on the cloth of a brilliant light. Man shall slumber when this occurs, so as to not interfere in the process. Man shall awaken to a new shining place. They shall see themselves as shimmering figures. Their step upon the land will feel as though they are walking on the clouds. They will see themselves as new. All past turmoil will seem petty and will not return into the new land.

Love shall be the rule of the new land. Man will not know of anything else. He will soon forget his past as he moves into the new life. Blessings onto this land and the new worlds that shall arise from her love.

December 11, 2003

Book of Gibraltar Part 2

You wonder why we again bring up this title. (Yes!) There is more to share in this document.

The sun, a most magnificent creature, was created to bring life to this planet and your fellow planets in this solar system. It changed its being to be the light and warmth to the planets that were brought here from other areas of this galaxy. Your sun, she holds the multiple points of light and sound that make up her structure. She glows with utmost splendor to spring life onto the surrounding planets. However, her structure is much more complex.

The sun is made up of many points of light that are felt on many dimensional levels. In the second, third, and fourth dimensional levels, she is viewed as a fiery ball. But in the higher dimensions, she shines her light not as a fiery ball, but as a lush life-filled paradise. Her inner sanctums are filled with life also. She knows her power and wields it with forces so great that she knows all movements are made by her and no other can move or shake her. She sends out vibrations that touch this world in such a way as to evoke life where new creations can make their way into the lower dimensions. Her decisions are a composite of forces, light and sound, that harmonize with the other stars that shine in this galaxy. Over one billion of these stars make up this universe. These forces of light form the matrix of life found in all of the worlds that inhabit this place. The web reaches out and into the fine threads of vibrations that man is able to see in his limited dimensions of second through fifth.

Her (the Sun's) currents create a bastion of releases the earth plane feels as heat. This enables the earth to spin on her axis at a rate within two decibels. The earth correlates her actions with that of the Sun so she can exist within this space and time. She receives her life from the frawns of the universe. Frawns are the fingers of life force that exist in all of the cosmos that reach into greater dimensions than man can realize. Man lives on only an infinitesimal part of the frawns. Life is much greater and extends into multitudes of experiences. It is always alive with new creations ever-expanding.

Knowledge of this shall bring man into a realized love that the Sun has for this planet. Into the further reaches of dimensional portals, the Sun is the gate where new creations can be viewed. She is able to provide this gate with her enormous abilities to shine her light into various dimensions to bring about the necessary accesses into the created worlds from which all new worlds exist. To reach the pinnacle of the new worlds, she proudly gives of herself in the moment to express a flow of rays that explode into one another. This breaks open a new gate (energy) for new expressions.

The complexity of this work is expressed in the warm glow of her outer rings. The energies burst into flame which gives earth her warmth and light. When the earth passes into a higher state of vibrations, then she will see through these fires into the great ball of life that the Sun is. She will be felt by her energetic stamp that she is much grander than a ball of gaseous substances. She knows of her-self and shall continue expressing her greatness and power to all who look upon her.

The final hour of her life in the solar system of Urion will be the time that her planets can rotate without her assistance. Her needs will change as all the planets move to their respective places in the cosmos. A beauty, the great ball of light is. With gratitude we send her our love from which she generates her life force.

January 18, 2004

Book of the Angelic Forces

This book has been handed down through many generations. Some of its text is part of **The Iliad.** *The great magnificent forces that we have termed Archangels have left their mark on this planet. Today they remain very close to humanity to bring an extended awareness to all life.*

Some see black and others see white. This is the dichotomy that exists on this planet Earth. An understanding of what existence means or "is" is the interpretation of each life form. The Earth is made up of a multitude of inhabitants. Some species stay for short periods of time while others remain through extended periods. One form that has remained on the planet is that form called the tree. Each tree has a life force that is a total of all the many inhabitants that make up its structure. The many plant forms, the many insect forms, and the many animal forms comprise the total tree. The tree receives its life, its strength from all of its parts. Each part or form gives of itself so the total of the sum of its parts is greater. Each has its own life to live yet each sapling becomes a large fortress with a trunk that reaches into its roots which binds itself with the soil and rocks. The branches reach out and produce food and become homes for the many forms. With the help of the Earth, the air, the water, and the Sun does the tree receive its full nourishment.

The Angelic Forces surround all humanity. They stretch out and touch all who will listen. They are here to bring peace and harmony among the peoples. They play an intricate part of revealing truth on this planet. Just like the tree, they reach out and encompass life in its many stages. They whisper truths in all life. Stop and listen and feel their presence.

Each Angel has its own attributes, its own set of energies. They are created to assist all of creation. They are an extension of the main force of creation. They work together and as teams. Their creation is still one of the mysteries of Creator Force. They have an incredible aptitude. They carry all truths but only to the extent of the matrix in which they inhabit. They inhabit more than one dimension simultaneously. They were created to be the hands of the divine. They bring forth the rings of creation, rings that make up the manifestation of life.

They have been dispensed to the earthly plane to assist this planet to evolve into an even greater spiral of evolution. The spirals of creation are the magnetic forces of the cosmos. All creation exists in the formation of these magnetic forces. The forces enable the lower creational forces establish new ways of Being the more physical dimensions, the dimensions of condensed light. Light within this spiral called the Creation Force of Adam has/is a dimension of extreme consciousness wavering inside the void. As the energy wavers, the angelic forces interject parts of their being into the "soup" to bring about balance. This balance is known as love in its highest degree. The love of the angelic forces, the Angels that bridge the arc between the lower to the higher dimensions comes from the heart of the One. The heart is the absolute love of itself.

The One is the tree. It is life made up of many species. It sends its roots into the lower dimensions and branches out into the heavens. It is an organism onto itself yet cannot live without the many living beings that make up its total being. It is life, it is energy. It knows of itself as One.

December 28, 2002

Book of Champions

True champions are ones who live with their truths, know their divine purpose, and extol their virtues. This book describes one such being. This took place in a small village on the outskirts of Chechnya, Yugoslavia.

Around the turn of the fifteenth century lived a boy who could talk with the animals. He had an uncanny sense about him that when he would gather his wits, the animals from the forest would gather around him. These animals of the forest could feel his love and devotion.

One day while toiling through the woods, a small deer approached the boy and wanted the boy to follow him. The boy excited about what the deer had to show him followed the deer deep into the woods. They came upon a bramble of bushes that lay low on the forest floor. Inside the brambles was a small animal with beady eyes and small pointed ears who was tangled in the vines. The small boy, seeing the animal in distress, freed it so it could continue on its path of just being an animal. The boy watched the animal scamper on its way down toward the river. The boy decided to follow anxious to see where the small animal was heading.

To the boy's amazement, the animal plunged into the river and swam under a rock. The small animal did not resurface and the boy was worried. Meanwhile the deer toiled about eating fresh greens to sustain its body. The boy looked at the deer and asked the deer if he should jump into the water to rescue the small animal. The deer, through its telepathic senses, told the boy, "No the small animal is not in any danger. It is just going home." The boy then became puzzled and asked the deer, "How does this small animal breathe if he is under water?"

The deer replied, "My friend, not all life is the same as yours. There are many animals of this kingdom that are able to live in the depths of water. Also, boy, do you not know that beneath this outcropping of rock that there is a cave hidden underneath it?"

The boy, sensing that a great mystery lies below them, plunged into the river looking for the opening to this wonderful cave. Almost out of breath, the boy happened upon a small opening. He could not get his body through the opening but he could see that a whole new world was before him as only his face could peer through the small opening in the rocks. He could see the small animal that he had rescued scampering about with the animal's small ones. What fun, he though, as he watched the animals play. The boy came up from this rock opening and noticed that his friend the deer was no-where in sight. He called out but the deer did not come to him. He then sat down upon an outcropping of rock and contemplated his whereabouts. He knew that the river was about a mile from his home. He saw that the current of the river flowed to his left and knew that, if he followed the river upstream, he would come upon a road that would lead him back to his home.

So the boy set out to go to his home. About this time, the skies were darkening. The boy did not worry about the darkness that was to befall him. He continued on his way until he came upon a small creek that flowed into the river. The boy thought "I can jump this stream." So the boy took a running start and jumped high but not far. He landed on a rock. The boy felt pain in his knee. He called out in pain. Soon the forest came alive with the animals coming out to help the boy. The small deer hearing the cry of the boy also came running to assist his friend. The deer walked into the shallow waters to the boy. The boy put his weight onto the deer's back to balance himself. The deer then walked with the boy supporting the boy as he walked. They continued on and reached the road to the boy's home. The deer, sensing that the boy could not walk without its assistance, stayed with the boy until the boy was safely home in his mother's arms.

Fear came across the face of the mother as she saw the deer with her son. Her reaction was to cause harm to the deer who she felt harmed her boy. But her son stopped her from striking the frightened animal. The boy exclaimed to his mother how the deer came to him so he could help a small animal in distress, then how the deer assisted him when he became distressed. The mother, sensing her frightened awareness, stopped and cried, realizing that her son fully trusted and knew that all is well and there is no reason to escape the beautiful wonders of the forest.

After that day, the mother with the help of her son planted a beautiful garden of flowers and vegetables which they shared with their animal friends. They came to know the animals and their families. They had no fear when the animals approached. They realized that the world is a place of total enjoyment and balance.

The boy lived to be over one hundred years old. He lived among his animal friends the whole time, just watching life in all its fullness. He wrote beautiful poems and stories about the forest. He had them chronicled into a series of stories that shall remain popular for generations to come.

He once wrote, "What is a champion?" "A champion is one who knows his boundaries but doesn't get stuck in that knowingness. He can fly, he can travel anywhere, any time, any place. Man has no limitations. Therein lies the greatest of champions."

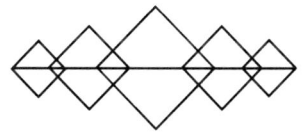

Q – Do we know the name of this boy and his great literary works?

A – His name is Leonard deVichot. He lived in the fifteenth century. He was well known in his small town. He liked to work with the small children. He held soliloquies to help his populace with the written word. He arranged for the learned ones to help with those who could not read or write. These schools became very popular with both men and women until the women were banned from higher learning. However the women continued to learn in the baskas where they bathed and cleaned their clothing.

January 25, 2003

Book of Salvation

The term "salvation" is used in many different ways. The phrase "to be saved" is an oxymoron, words that are not spoken in the higher dimensions. The term "to be saved" means that you are taken from someone or something. How can that be when you are part of Creator God, All That Is? This book shall help many people find the true meaning of the word "salvation" as it is used in the many texts of your Bible.

During my incarnation as Yeshua ben Joseph, I spoke about this very thing upon The Mount. That speech/teaching has been rewritten many times but with added twists which has strayed away from the true intent and meaning of the teaching. A pure copy of this service can be found upon the rocks located in the mountain of "the tender."

Before Sananda spoke, I could see his muscular legs and the hem of his natural beige clothing wrap. I could tell he was speaking to a group of people that had gathered. Perhaps this vision says that he is rooted to this Earth or our rooting here on Earth is in the physical. The words "the tender" also has many meanings such as the keeper. Look within your heart for its meaning to you.

My staff assists me on my walks. I use it for guidance, to move obstacles from my path. When my path is clear I will have no more need of this wonderful tool. That, my friends, is the path to God. Before all of you are tools. They assist you in the marketplace, your living quarters, your journeys as your traverse the countryside. In nature, these tools are freely given. But when you feel your bodies move differently upon this plane, you will have no need for such tools.

Yes, you will still see the beauty in the rocks, in the waters, and in the wilderness. You will become a part of them and they a part of you. You will see their true beingness. And you will know who your own true being is. Speak of the moments where you find yourselves inexplicably wrapped around the tall trees. You feel their pulse, and their being lights up with your love. Feel the blades of grass upon which you sit. Can you feel their life? Those of you who are sitting upon the great rocks, can you feel their pulsing? Life exists in everything. When you are one with all, then you will be in gratitude of all you see. The tools of your journey shall become a part of you. You will cast down all transgressions. You shall feel the oneness. You will find that all life is to share. What beautiful beings you all are incarnate in the flesh, God in the flesh. Not only am I God, so are you.

Be it to each and every one of you. Walk in this world and feel the God (Source) in all you feel, see, hear, taste, and smell. Know the wonders of Creation. This knowing of the wonder that lives within each one of you, each blade of grass, each tall tree, each pebble on which you walk, and each rock on which you sit shall be known as your greatest works. Your children will carry on these creations. Create in love and you shall be love.

My Father, your Father, begins new creations with every breath we take. Look into each one's eyes that are seated with you. Peer deeply into the eyes and you shall find absolute love. Know this love in your hearts. Cast aside all tools for you will not have need of these in the new world.

Just as I am a wayshower, shall you be. Walk and speak with total assurance. Love all your brothers and sisters, all animals for their gifts, and all plants for their wondrous gifts of food. We rock into a new time and place of God assurance that all is divine, there is no other way. I now lay down my staff for it has been of great comfort, but no longer serves me. Your paths lie before you. Step into the knowing of the great divine Source.

February 14, 2003

(64)

Book of Forgiveness

In the times to come, many seek to cleanse themselves of all fear, hate, jealousy, and all darkness that will hold them back from their attaining ascension. This book deals with the many situations that occur and steps to clear oneself of these inner demons.

This book was written before my birth as Jeshua, approximately 100 BC. It can be found within the walls of Canaan, the temple which holds some of the ancient writings of Israel.

Blind we are in the becoming of the masters that we all seek. Believe in yourselves, your own master that you hold within. Connect your wisdom to that of the divine force of all good, that of holy God.

Blend your will of the forces of good and evil, and there you will find a balance that will hold and sustain you in the physical life. Enact a program that will nourish your soul yet leave you with an imbalance of knowledge. To know yourself as good, you shall know evil. Do not hold yourselves in that place where you only perceive demons. They are there for you to realize your existence. Speak to them of love and you will see them quickly disappear. Hold with your vision the feelings of peaceful love and your soul shall rest. Desperate situations are there for you only to project your consciousness that you need a rest, the world needs a rest. Civilizations are built upon such unrest. They seek the balance. Thus you could say that evil is a precursor to higher evolution.

This planet called Earth stands for the truth of divine justice. On this planet are the many peoples of many past civilizations as well as other planets that are here to join all nations into One. It has been decreed that all will come to an understanding that all life everywhere is but an extension of Creator in its many forms.

Do unto others as you would do unto yourself. Treat others divinely for they are divine just as you are. True justice comes from your willingness to create in love for the love of Creator. When you feel that divine connection (you could not be anything else), go into your hearts and feel that energy permeate your total beings and extend that feeling out into this world, this cosmos. When you do this, you are extending God through the myriad forms created by the mind of God.

The power of God's mind, which is your mind, seeks a level of total balance in the formation of life. Truth means that you are the only creator of your own world. Existence is only your perception of your world. This world, this planet Earth, has planted her seed for the deliverance of man into a new world of peaceful tranquility. To obtain this tranquility is to submit to Creator God love and compassion to all life. Thus with this compassion will all life be in total balance. As you peer through your eyes, look into all eyes deep into the soul of your brother. In each person lies a wondrous entity of love creation. Be silent to hear their inner voices sing in holy harmony. You are the chorus that creates this harmony. You are your brother and you are your sister. You are everlasting life. Breathe deeply in this matrix of creation. The many parts of yourself shall make manifest the whole of creation. You shall discover all of your roots and know the existence that you really are.

Speak only of good for goodness shall set your free. See only goodness and that is what you shall receive. All dark corners that have existed in your beings shall diminish and the light shall set you free. Oh Creator Gods of this universe, sing your songs of love and the chorus that you create shall lift you higher into the heavenly hosts. You shall create in new and wondrous ways. You are wondrous beings built only with love.

We leave you with this knowledge that all is built into this exquisite being called Creator God. You each are a part of the whole. Manifest love like you have never manifested love before. Memories shall resurface. You will become balance. You will understand life in its fullness.

Namaste, from your "higher" selves speaking to you in all your forms.

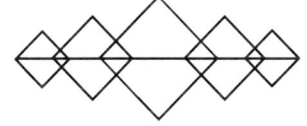

You have manifested both love and hate. Love is the only life to live because hate is only that feeling of uneasiness, of non-connections. Release all doubts and fears. They are there for you to know that they are not real. They cannot sustain themselves where the love of Creator exists. Do you understand?

There is not evil. There is no devil. There is no one outside of yourselves to deceive you. The concept of Hell is only a concept. In reality it does not exist. Only in living your lives do you go through the concept of hell – not being in the feeling of life flow. The flow of life exists only with love. Know this and only speak of this for truly you are God in many expressions.

February 23, 2003

Book of Deeds

During the recession of the 1920s, as well as the era of repressed knowledge or Cataclins, rose an interest in mental telepathy. People around the world had a thirst for the paranormal. They knew that existence was beyond what they could see. They drew their knowledge on the work of Aristotle, the one known as the Father of Math and Science of the Universe.

This book is a book of numbers. The number five is a curious number in that it cannot be divided by any whole number. Thus we have a situation where whole numbers can be divided into segmented numbers or fractions. Our planet rotates in a circle on an axis. We can count the stars and know by their positions precisely what the hour is and what day in our cycles. You ask what does the number five divided into fractions have to do with our planet rotating on its axis?

Take the integer of five, divide it by 2 and you get 2.5. Divide 2.5 by 2 and you get 1.25. When you continue dividing these integers, you finally reach the number .078125. This is the number of the stars. Within our galaxy lies a multitude of stars, each planet rotating in a similar manner of our dear Terra. Within the framework of our galaxy can we hypothesize that the number .078125 is our relationship and position to the center of the universe. Theoretically, when we combine our planetary existence with all the other planets in this galaxy, we find that the planets' positions form a triad of multiple planes each separate in their identity, yet relate in the sphere of all.

Bounce two balls with the same density, at the same heights, and with the same force, and the balls shall bounce at the same velocity and heights. When you take one of the balls and take away half of its density, and bounce it from the same height, with the same force, then the less dense ball will bounce twice as high as the dense ball. Such is our universe. Our beloved Terra wishes to take her place in this universe as a spinner of webs, each web varying in its density.

Within each of the five webs that surround our planet is a pattern of vibrations that relate to each of the five lower dimensions. Thus you can say that our Terra exists in all five dimensions simultaneously. As she spins on her axis, each of the webs vibrate at a different rate. The sound of this interplay of dimensions harmonizes and acts as a beacon to others in the universe. The play of this harmonic coincides with the positioning of our planet within the structure of the universe, thus the number .078125 reveals itself in the formation of the divine plan of the universe.

When man harmonizes with the same tonal quality and frequency, can he reach into other areas of our universe as well as the five dimensions of Terra.

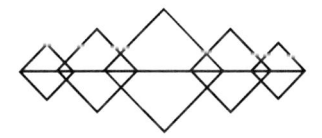

Q – Explain why this book is called "Book of Deeds."
A – A deed is that which is an agreement achieved. Your earth, also known as Terra, agreed to be part of the lower five dimensions before her moving into the higher dimensions of creatorship.

Note: I was told the number five is equivalent to freedom.

In time you will more fully understand this book and its discussions on numbers.

Q – What does this book have to do with mental telepathy?

A – The interplay of the five dimensions or five webs gives ones the ability to tap into all of these dimensions just by concentration and focus of the heart/mind. Wherever you put your focus, shall you be transported into a new timeline.

Q – Timeline?

A – All dimensions hold different timelines or planes of existence.

March 16, 2003

Book of the Light Ship Athena

Aboard the Star Ship Athena is a fascinating aspect of physicality. We all come here for respite and to glance at other civilizations throughout the universe. This ship enables us to glaze the universe in all of its aspects by use of our technology. Welcome aboard!

Welcome to our ship! You all have been here before and some of you visit often although you may not be aware of your visits. We invite you to come and join with us and see consciously what you have been doing on the inner planes.

We have been in existence for what you would term thousands of years. We can go in and out of time zones, which means we can either go forward in your Earth years or back to ancient times. We note that there will be a change in the frequencies in which you live. Memories of your existences on earth and other planets may surface with our progression through this ship.

As you stand in the holding area, you may note a pulsing sensation. This ship does breathe as it is alive and part of us. We integrate our existence into the very shell of this ship. It has life, it is life. Stretch your minds into that space where your world comes to a rest. Reach into your higher selves and feel the energy emanating from your being. This will help you connect to that part of you that recognizes where you are. We shall move on into the inner sanctums of the ship.

On your left you will see a series of half round arches with pink light emanating through them. These chambers are for the integration of peaceful love. Let your bodies feel the softness of this light. Let it permeate through your systems. Look around and you will see many others relaxing, being cleansed and feeling much warmth. There are many assistants to help you with your clearings. When your bodies feel rejuvenated, please move to the outer lounge area where you can sip the clean waters especially prepared for you.

As you look around, you will see walkways that are much like laser beams. They are safe for you to walk on. You will note that these beams are in one of three colors – blue, green, and yellow-gold. Each color/frequency has its own agenda in that, with your intent, the paths will lead you where you want to go.

This ship serves many species of life, most of which can be found on Mother Earth. Yet we also house other beings of the bird and animal kingdoms that are not found on your planet. Plant life flourishes in the agricultural chamber as well as placed throughout the ship. New species are grown as research for the plant's impact upon the environment. Understand that we are able to grow infinite varieties of plants because many of the plants are multidimensional and will flourish under various light frequencies. Many of the species that thrive on earth are first tested in this chamber, then released to planet Earth.

Another chamber that is very important to those of you on Earth is the Chamber of Recollections. In this chamber, human entities can scan their own biology to remember the reasons why they had incarnated into a family lineage. Also one can scan their soul family for information that may assist them in their current incarnation. To visualize their past incarnations can sometimes be quite overwhelming so we require that one does not spend too much of their visit in this chamber.

The Health and Healing Chamber works on a multitude of levels. Upon entering this chamber, one passes through an archway made up of colored rainbow lights. Soft music plays in the background. If one of your species is toxic, which most humans are, that person will be seated in the detox room in which various lights will vibrate through the biology and neutralize the toxins. The next room one would enter is the Body Scan Room. The ethereal body or aura is checked for any deficiencies. Then various lights and sounds are applied to boost the body's immune system. Finally the body is to rest before it can continue on in the ship.

The Control Room is located in the upper levels of the ship. This chamber is reserved for the masters who understand the many levels of propulsion in the grids that are throughout the universes. These engineers must understand the dynamics of the interplay of magnetics built into the systems of biologic energies of the cosmos.

There are a total of 165 types of chambers in this ship. The ones that are most interesting to the Earth human are described above. When humans are ready to expand their awareness', they will understand the Chambers of Gratitude and Release. These chambers are reserved for those who are ready to move their awareness to the realms of higher existence. This chamber helps clear the way for a soul to move on into the nonmaterial realms. Attachment to a body is released and the golden energy spirals into an existence that is beyond the lower seven physical dimensions.

The divine plan is for all humans to traverse through the lower dimensions into the higher states of being. Creation exists on so many levels and those levels are constantly expanding. The Creative forces of this Universe are moving in a spiral into new manifested heavens.

This book shall be left within the confines of Library of Delphin.

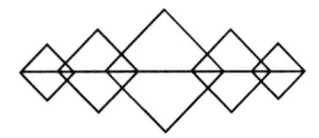

Q – Is the Light Ship Athena part of the Ashtar Command?

A – This ship is used by the Ashtar Command as one of its main or mother ships.

Q – Please explain who is the Ashtar Command and why they are here to support the earth and humanity.

A – It is I, Ashtar, who wishes to speak. We come from a mixture of galaxies, planets, and life forms. We select those beings who are on this ship who want to support humanity on its mission to be part of the Light of God in Creatorships. We work with the planet Earth, helping the planet in her stabilizations, clearing of debris on and within her, and the humans who call upon us for support. We have multitudes of ships that surround your planet. Many do see us, yet we remain invisible to most human eyes. We work with many of the Masters who have incarnated upon the Earth plane. We continue these relationships today. Our attire is skin suits as most of us look very much human. Many of us have large eyes and small mouths. We communicate telepathically and also with our voices just as most humans do. We have been involved with many activities on earth, such as adjustments in some of your weather patterns. However, we do not interfere with many of your weather patterns at this time so the humans can play out their life patterns.

Our ships are on alert at all times. Before the vibration of Earth was in the fourth dimension, we volunteered to support all humans and worked with other beings and their ships as long as they did no harm to their subjects. However, there were abductions that went on by millions of people. Some people have remembrances of these abductions. But at this moment on this timeline, there can be no more abductions or experiments with the animals and humans by off-world beings.

With much gratitude, we salute all beings on this Earth at this time. This is such a momentous occasion because humanity decided to come forth in power to be the gods of tomorrow.

July 6, 2003

Book of the Templars

It is time for the information that has been kept secret by the Templars be revealed for all of humanity. The secret codes and passages that have been sealed within the chambers by those who hold them sacred shall be opened and the ancient wisdom shared. This wisdom has already been revealed to the masses but in much a different way. No longer shall the key be hidden. It is time.

It is within this Earth that mysteries of the ancients are hidden. These secrets shall stay within the confines of the holy church until such time that the church falls and can no longer contain the secrets. The Holy Grail of Jerusalem is the passage of man into the bowels of Earth. Here the masters of old reside, defining what, where, and when the momentum of the stars and their effects on the human body shall mutate into the persona of divine grace and magnitude that is destined for the earth plane.

The great mysteries of man and animal are stored in what is the final hour of the Holy Plan. Man shall resurrect into a new being of fine internal power. Glory abounds as the light enters into its final phase of everlasting life. All trials and tribulations shall be finished with the new day, the new time, the new way of life. The sacred light held within these bowels shall make its way into the eternal flame of understanding. The mysteries of this light have been held by The Brotherhood. This sect of divine brothers has formed the cross of the

Holy Flame over the portal of the divine feminine. With the cross of both the masculine and the feminine, the balance of life's energy is the balance of the flame within the flame. The ones of old shall make of themselves into the new body and skin of the young. They shall leave of their homes within the bowels and rise into the outer regions of this great magnificent star of the heavens. These great ones have been the protectors of this vast world, vast in Earth's harboring of life on many levels and planes.

The rivers run wide and take the flow of the magnetic forces into the seas. The stillness that lies at the bottom of the great seas holds the energies of Terra/Gaia in the place of protection of her interiors. The Brotherhood assists in this protection of her great light. For the Brotherhood have assisted in the internal web of the electromagnetic forces. They have used their co-creative light to weave this web to connect this Earth in this solar system of Mais *(Ma – iz)*.

Buildings shall be erected to help hold these energies where there is no edifice or rock (crystals) in these chakra locations in the Earth. The ones who hold these secrets, those who are the Templars, know of this and shall obey the Universal Laws of Oneness in their daily lives. They shall guide the peoples in their divine powers given to them. The church shall know of this and keep it from the masses until such time all people can exercise their powers in the protection of Earth and the magnificence She holds. The growth of mankind shall continue until they, too, realize that they are One with Creator and all existence is the work of God in all its forms.

The intertwining flames of the inner and outer worlds will rise as One flame in the eternal moment of gestation. The Templars divine decree shall be carried out in precision. The temples in which they build shall be fortresses that connect the sacred patterns of creation.

In the holy name of the Christ, their work shall live on until the end of time. The holy one of Bethlehem will make himself known at this end of time. He will show the peoples of their heritage, their beginnings. He shall lead the church until the people lead their selves. He is of the Brotherhood, the Masters of this place, this world. He who finds these truths shall know that, indeed, it is the end of time.

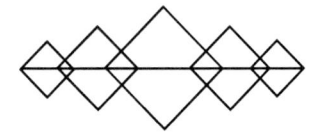

After writing this book, I saw the symbol of the solar cross.

Q – Who is the holy one of Bethlehem who is to make himself known at this end o f time?

A – The Holy ONE is God himself/herself within all of creation. Man shall realize and is realizing that they all are part of the One.

Note that the name Bethlehem means "House of the Lord." See the book "Book of the Road to Beth-Le-Hem."

Q – What is meant by: "the rivers run wide and take the flow of the magnetic forces into the seas"?

A – The term rivers are the magnetic lines of the earth that flow into the crystalline structures, many of which are under water in your oceans.

Q – This solar system has been name "Urion" in the Book of Gibraltar, Part 2. In this book, our solar system is called "Mais." Please explain.

A – The name "Mais" is the name given to this solar system by the ones who came here and were known as the Elohim. The name "Mais" means strength. The Spanish term for corn is "maiz" which means strength given through food. The word "maize" is an American name for yellow corn which has many uses and benefits.

The name "Urion" is a cosmic name given this solar system by the creator gods of Abraham. Urion simply comes from the connections in this solar system, the cosmic energies or particles.

This solar system is known by many names depending on which group of beings you are communicating with.

July 13, 2003

Book of the Holy Sepulcher

This book of The Holy Sepulcher is not about my birthplace or place of physical death, but a place in The Holy Land that is the center of the birth of separateness. This place is about the tides of yesterday where man saw himself as lowly and alone. He did not see himself as the great power that he is. These writings live among those held by the Vatican. They have been transcribed yet not understood. They sit in a vault protected by the church personages. They shall be found and read to the masses. There will be many translations but know that the only true translation is the one of love, brotherhood, and obedience to the word of God in the name of Christ. He who lives by the Universal Laws of the One is living the life of Christ. I was one such being. I taught this concept and lived it in my later life. I am known as the one of servitude to both my father and my mother. I am the alpha and the omega, yet I live on. You, too, are the alpha and the omega and you will live on.

These words are to be read and heard with an open heart and an open mind. On these scrolls are written the symbols of power. Man shall find his way home, home to the internal love of Spirit. This Spirit resides in all of man yet the powers of this world lead the people blindly until they cannot see, nor hear, nor know the infinite wisdom that they possess. They shall continue with their lives full of remorse yet they do not know where this remorse comes from. They believe that the Holy Land of this world is the place of God, yet he is the one who leads his people into darkness. This one who they call in the Tales of Woe is the mastermind of this place, the cave of Babel. Within these caves are the passages of the Kings. The Kings rule this area with the force of the mighty sword and who have little regard for the human life. Yet these Kings are worshipped for their power and magnificence which they display.

These Kings take it upon themselves to rule with the golden spire. Their magic brings a spell to the people. The laws of the day are written in the books of old that have been kept within the confines of the church. These laws submit unto a god, the god of Elijah, the god of Nathan, and the god of Israel. This god of infinite passion has ruled the people in their tales of woe that started a sacrificial time to appease the other gods.

The God of Abraham, the source of all power, has been usurped for the reaping of the gods of Turan. Their spell shall last until the people take their own power unto themselves. The people's lives as slaves to these beings are in concordance to the writings of the Bekeleh.

Hear now that all sons and daughters are born within this place with the agreement that all shall be freed unto the light. The people shall be taught that all love stems from the main creator source. Within this light, man shall carry on with his toil until he realizes that this toil is his choosing. Man, in his righteousness, shall return to the time when all was equal, when all was the garden of love. This magnificent body of Earth has within its body the means for transformation into the star of Jerusalem. This body of Earth is a mechanism that can transmit itself into the heavens of love where all life is dependent upon itself.

To those people who reside here in this Holy Land. The land has been torn asunder. The caves have been built to house the nobility of those who seek to rule the people so that they are subservient to the false god. The area known as The Holy Sepulcher, is the passage into these caves. They mark the entrance into the dark ages.

The Holy Land is the birthplace of thought of original existence. There are many who have come through this portal to be a part of this earthen structure. These beings come to this planet of self-realization to bring their gifts of power to a land that has been used and abused by past civilizations. The beauty of all civilizations is that the many forms that have contributed to creation use this life force to learn and move on to greater and greater forms of co-creation. The missive shall turn their power over to others that want to rule. Soon all will become rulers. All life that exists with this planet Earth will have the option of new creation or stay within the confines of slavery. All choices are honored. Each life form has its own path of living life. The golden spire lives within all who want to see and use it for their highest good. All magic resides within each life. All is beauty.

The Holy Land shall part its waters in making the new land and leaving the old patterns as they are. This portal that has been open shall turn and the entrance shall close on itself. To those who wish to see shall see. Those who wish to hear shall hear. Those who wish to know shall know. All life moves in a pattern called love.

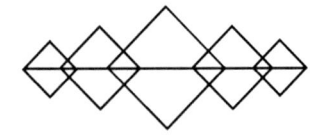

The symbol shown is The Flower of Life.

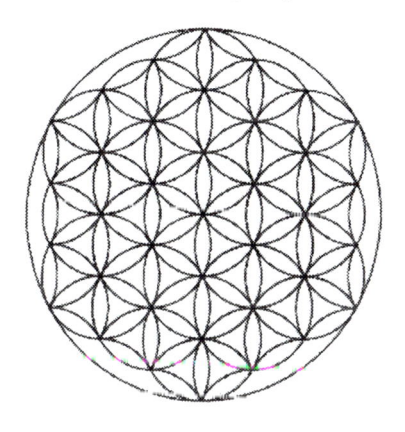

Q – In the first paragraph it is written, "he is the one who leads his people into darkness." Who is "he"? God as stated in the beginning of the sentence?

A – The statement that it is God is correct, but not Creator God or the heart of God. Remember all is God for it can be no other way. In that time, the people were ruled by kings who felt they were chosen by God. In truth, they chose themselves because of their abilities to perform what many people thought were miracles. What the people did not know was that these kings knew how to manipulate matter. They were alchemists. But in their experiments, they proved their abilities with the use of iron and magnetism. Since the people did not know about the magnetic forces, they gave their power to the kings. The kings enjoyed their control but misused it to benefit themselves. They introduced slavery and servitude to themselves.

Q – What is the golden spire?

A – The kings built great edifices proclaiming their own divinity by use of the spire wrapped in gold atop of their buildings.

Q - In the first sentence of the last paragraph, it is said, "the Holy

Land shall part its waters in the making of the new land" followed by, *"and leaving the old patterns as they are."* Please explain.

A – The counting of the days that shall precede the sinking of the land and closing of the portal is imminent and happening now. This land shall perish covering the unrest that has taken place there. Please note that the waters come to balance or wash the once arid land so that all the suffering and abuse of human kind shall perish with it. Know that this is the time when all is being cleansed. All is being made new, including our thought patterns. Being made new is moving away from the old thought patterns of separateness. That part of your soul lives is almost finished. And each of you has made it so.

Jerusalem: Being the balance of the masculine and feminine.

See "Book of the Nightingale" for more information on the gods of Turan and the writings of the Bekeleh.

February 23, 2004

The Apple Tree

In the far reaches, man has sought to understand nature and the food line. He was taught to fear what is rightfully his. He was frightened in reaching for the fruit of life. All fruit is made for the expression of regeneration. Regeneration is there for all to partake. You will always be offered what is rightfully yours. Note the difference from taking what belongs to another. There will always be enough on this planet to house and feed all beings. This story about the apple tree was written many thousands of years ago when man was experimenting with genetic engineering in the formation of various types of life. Namaste.

Malleable. That what it takes to feed the mouth of those who walk in the foot-steps of this mighty Earth. Within this Earth are the seeds for future generations. They have been placed within the ground to feed the hunger of life. Man shall know of its use as they will observe the animals, the birds that shall teach man to fly.

Within the bowels of Earth shall rise the mighty fortresses. Each seed shall break forth from the ground and grow into the heavens. Upon this mighty fortress shall the masses be fed and housed. Within this earthen structure shall the seed break forth and become the tree. The tree shall bear fruit and this fruit shall be as food for the peoples. The energy of fruit shall bring nourishment to the bodies, the physical part of creation.

The light shall be as food to nourish the cells (the component parts) of the body. It becomes the body until its energy is lost (transmuted). It is part of the cycle of life. It knows of itself and gives freely of itself.

The stamen of the seed gathers the light, the moisture, the nutrients of the crystals of the Earth. As these are absorbed, regeneration begins. The outer flesh is broken down as it is absorbed by beings or returned to the dust of the Earth. The seeds are then free to drop back into the boughs of the Earth.

The beauty of such an interchange of energy shall keep beings in their physicalness. Their wont of energy to propel their bodies will be part of their survival of physicality. All beings are to understand that they are to be the caretakers of this grand energy. They shall respect the Earth for her part in this manifestation.

We are those who work with condensed matter. We work with the cosmic forces to bring about an exchange of love. We do this to bring about a balance upon this Earth and this part of this solar system. The needs are great to change this station from one of greed to one of love. The apple is our symbol of love. Freely use of its light and respect Mother Earth as it transcends the weight of darkness. Earth's beauty will reach out and touch the many who will make it their mission to bring about balance of the cosmic forces. When eating of the fruit of the apple, give thanks to Mother Earth as she grows into cosmic adulthood. We create in love as One.

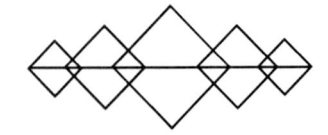

Symbol called Core Energy

April 5, 2004

The Right of Dawn

Before the coming of the ancient ones you call the Lemurians, there existed on this Earth a throng of beings who worked within the waters below the lands. They left their gift. The gifts are in the Earth today.

The nautilus, the spiral of creation has within it secrets of the worlds. It contains vertebrae that read of times past and times future. It knows itself as the spiral of evolution. It creates within itself. These species are to grow in number as they expand the awareness of the species that reside here on this land as well as the life that will inhabit this orb.

The knowledge of all creation can be seen, felt, heard within the scope of the ninth layer of being. It resembles the life force that spirals in all directions in the cosmos. The sec-spiral releases its spin and continues both in and out. It crosses itself as the spin makes a circular movement. Life is unending.

The spiral connects itself through the threads that attach its many layers. The threads run vertically. Therefore, life is vertical. There is no past and there is no future. Life just continues. As the spiral meets itself, the vibrations increase, become stronger. They pulse at a rate that pushes the spiral through the higher frequencies. Time will act as if it blends itself across the lines appearing linear. The earth will be in a zone that measures its place in the cosmos and its interactions within itself.

The species of the nautilus will imbed itself within the rock, the solidified dust. It will be a time-table to present the idea of space within space. It precedes itself in the heavens. The great bodies of condensed oxygen and hydrogen will serve as the material in which the nautilus shall thrive. It will become as the temple of the spirit, just as the spirit moves through all spirals of creation. It is the force of the All. All creatures will recognize their place, their spiral, as they merge upon the lands. The shapes and figures will be catalyzed thought. The band of frequencies of the lower octaves will consume the images of Bak-tan, the form of thought in motion. The form shall be as an interpreter of thought. It is the dawn of creation of the lower octaves. The imprints are there for all to see, recognize their larger creation.

The beginning of the nautilus in form is a way for mankind to understand creation. Representations of unending life is portrayed in the hardened shells. The deliverer of the form is through the mechanism of the ditrad, the form used to move the circular energies into a solidified frequency. The form becomes hardened so the spiral and its connective tissue can be seen and felt by the lower band of frequencies of mankind on Earth. This is an experiment to see if the lower kingdoms can disseminate creation that exists. This is another way for creation to know of itself on all levels. Even the make up of these spirals is to be a part of this understanding. The thought forms of this new creation are in place and shall be protected by the ones of the seventh galaxy. These masters can bring in assistance from other galaxies as long as they do not interfere in this evolutionary process. This experiment is a precursor to the much larger process of the cosmic forces coming into balance. This is a new way for creation to know that all possibilities exist simultaneously. What is learned here shall affect the whole. The cosmic forces of the Omniverse will be shown in ways to be expanded upon. The new waves of creation are moving out in all directions and are to be felt in all levels of being. Within this newly-made sphere will the representation of All Life Force be ingrained in all the octaves of manifestation. The tones of manifestation are set. The elements of time are in place and shall be as the record of life. The waves are being sent to begin the process. Once set, then the process will build upon itself. Gratitude or the knowledge of this movement shall keep the process in action and level upon level will be obtained. To the great Ones who have caused this movement, we extend our love. Let this love in motion begin.

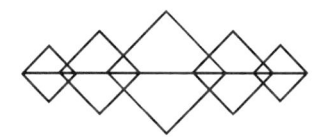

Q – What is the ninth layer of being?

A – This refers to the mankind or humankind in the forceps of the Father. This is another way of saying that man is a part of creation creating in his own image.

Q – Please explain more about the ditrad, the form used to move the circular energies of the nautilus or spiral into a solidified frequency.

A – The ditrad is an energy made up of a series of pulses that give a form that looks like a double helix. Your DNA is very much the ditrad form. Energy pulses (electron network produces this flow) cascade through the connective filaments within the sec-spiral (sec- meaning sections within the whole). Di means the entering of the positive and negative electrical currents of your electromagnetic system *(in the dictionary, the prefix "di" means double)*, and trad means to traverse. A solidified frequency is just frequency slowed down in which man or an object appears to be solid.

August 10, 2003

Book of the Siege

The time of Eurocles was a major transition of the world and her peoples. The people of that era gathered together in the name of the chosen one, the one who would rule the world. His name was Maltan and he came to this planet to restore order. He brought with him an army of beings who had the technology to bring about the changes in the topography of the lands. His strength was apparent to all who were in his presence. He had mastered the means to move energy to benefit the peoples. His knowledge in the preservation of the many species who inhabited the earth at that time was the original intent for his coming to this planet. Here is his story.

I have been called to be a part of this transformation of this planet. I volunteer to come, to live, to understand this part of the cosmos. I come in the light of the everlasting love, patience that is known as the force of the almighty matrix of the One Kingdom. This portion of the divine matrix is one of the places that shall endure the hardships of biology. The many webs that have been built to be a part of this planet bring a new dimension to the Kingdom. The forces that have left this planet have created a tear in the time web that encompasses this solar system. The mighty light of Sun washes upon this jewel who has inhabited this solar system in her training to be a magnificent shining star, a point in the matrix of the One Kingdom that can hold and direct the waves of divine knowledge and opportunity for other parts of this One Kingdom in the building of new Kingdoms.

    I bring my army of cellular mass to grow on this planet. They shall absorb the internal light that is within this planetary body. As they absorb this light, they shall awaken to the mass knowledge of the universe, the One Kingdom. They shall evolve to a power much greater than I. I, too, shall grow to a much greater power. The matrix shall grow and all life can traverse this matrix. It shall be the way to everlasting evolution.

    We shall spin a new web to hold into place the life forms that have gathered here on and in this planet. We shall work with the mind/personality of this planet to bring about a balance to her body. She, too, shall awaken from her pain as she transcends into a greater light. All frequencies of this body shall attune to the forces held within Sun. They are the light bearers whose job it is to direct the electromagnetic forces to hold into place the great planets of this solar system. All of these planets shall hold their forces in place as they work together to form an accompanying system of solar bodies. Movement of this solar system will begin to gravitate to an area in the great matrix called The Cross of Orion. This brings about a conjunction of three great systems, two of which are ready for this conjunction. My job is to bring this solar system into balance, to assist in making it ready for the grand conjunction. Others shall inhabit the other planetary bodies of this solar system to ready them. The mighty conjunction shall bring about a force of such a magnitude that a new heaven shall rise.

    My people, ready yourselves to bring about the stabilization of this planet. Stabilize all forces of this grand lady. Work with the masters of Sun and the eleven planets of this solar system.

With this, the grand cycle has begun. In the light of the One Kingdom, I AM Eurocles. We are the grand masters who have come in planetary service.

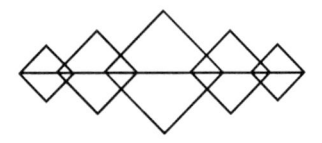

Q - I thought evolution was always "everlasting." So what is meant by the second paragraph?

A – God or Infinite Spirit has what is called the in-breath and the out-breath. The in-breath refers to creating and the out-breath is the manifestation of that creation. What has not been said that this creation has an alpha (beginning) and an omega (ending). The evolution of this creation has been an experiment for Creator (Infinite spirit). This creation was set to implode on itself, or, in essence, that it never existed. But with divine interplay, the love quotient was brought back in and expanded upon. This great expansion, which is happening now, from the 1930s on, has brought Earth's civilizations to the forefront of all civilizations because of this influx of love. Therefore those beings, human and others of similar make-up, are to be the forerunners of new and expanded creations. Many will be thought of as gods in these new creations. They are as gods because these new civilizations will be of their own making. And this was Infinite spirit's intention.

Q – In the third paragraph, which three great systems are included in the grand conjunction?

A – Orion, Sirius, and the Pleiades.

Siege: any prolonged or persistent endeavor to overcome resistance: a long period of distress, illness, or trouble.

November 17, 2003

Book of the Seven

I see the inside of a cave. I see a passageway around both sides of a rock as it balances the huge boulder and earth that lies above it. It is light where I stand but darkness is at the door of the passageway.

You see the entrance into a place where there are the documents to the Holy Grail. There are the remains of the Tree of Avalon. The tree is a set of books that were written upon my arrival to the Seines. There is a truth that is known by many yet not released to the general populace. It is the holy word of the ancients that preceded written word as you have known it. The symbols are quite extraordinary and can quite easily be interpreted. This line of teaching is the truth spoken two thousand years ago. My balance partner held my place in the city of Judea while I continued on my journey in the northern lands. Please continue speaking the truth. More chaos will come because of this truth, but it quickly will turn to freedom in the days ahead.

The light, that substance that makes up all life, shall pervade this beautiful Earth. Her cry to bring balance to her being was answered. She knows of her making and her inheritance. Yet she breathes a fine mist into her being to bring forth life upon her surface. The coalescing of matter into form is made possible with the thoughts of our brethren, those of us who have the spirit of the blinding force. This force is so powerful that it exists within all physical life.

To the elders who have come before me, who have taught the seven stages of life, you have served the Creator Force with your brevity and knowledge that all life is the moment. It breathes a song, a melody of love. When heard and felt by our lady, this great Earth, new forms of life erupted upon the surface. The interchanging forces of life brought forth the continuation of magnetism into a form of expanding life. The gears of the force are within the Creator force itself, in the particles, the waves, in the magnetism, in the electricity made from the poles established by this magnetism. It is a grand force made with the holy hands of love.

Our mission is to bring about the continuation of this holy Force so that it is understood by all life forms. It is whole unto itself but must be made into containments of power to express itself. This power is for all and is all. Therefore it can be molded into any form that one wishes. When balance is not attained, then the form shall dissipate as it cannot hold anything but balance.

Man and woman were made to bring a balance to this land of plenty. Each are made with their respective parts to be whole unto themselves but also to come together to explore each part of a balance. They were made to mutate themselves in continuing life forms as man and woman. The messages of the adam, the eve or uva are the procreativity of life. The egg shall inherit the balance to bring physical life into the next moment. Our brothers and sisters of the stars know of this and shall be a part of this process. Their knowledge of these processes of life shall be a part of understanding the polarities of the balance.

The elders have left their knowledge of balance for this continuation of life on beautiful Terra. They leave their mark on the stone tablets given to our master that has come before, our beloved Master Melchizedek. Their words (symbols) were

to give us guidance to understand ourselves. The symbols can be interpreted to mean:
1. The force of life is One force.
2. Creator's hands, the One force, are your hands.
3. Mountains are made, the seas are made for the life of Gaia, her Terra.
4. Knowledge is in seat of all Force, to be used in the making of all things.
5. Right, left, up, down are only polarities to experience.
6. Life can only sustain itself with balance.
7. Create in fullness, create in balance, create in love.

All things made new are made by you. With the grace or love within the One Force, all is possible but only in the balance. We pray to understand and we understand to pray. Our prayer, our thoughts are what we are made up of. Nothing can take these away from us. In this grand moment, I AM THAT I AM. Recognize the life in all, see its grandness, and understand that joy is the product of this understanding. The teaching of the One is now complete. Know of its simplicity, know of its freedom, and know of its love.

February 8, 2004

The Fall from Grace

These writings are for humanity to understand who he is, where he is going, and what he can expect in this lifetime as well as other lifetimes. Man is the generator of the next revolution of the stars. Man is here to bring about a change in the whole sequence of spiritual integration. Man is life that is unfolding into a nuclear fusion of new life which will affect all creation. Do not think that you are just small creatures having a life on this planet. It is much more than that. Understand the importance of this time, this day in which humanity will stand up and be noted as the cosmic force. My love to all man. May he see with his own eyes, the inner eye of God, in the unfolding of new life. Live each and every day with new eyes, new breath, and observe yourselves as well as others. Soon you will comprehend your magnificence.

Hear now the ringing of the bells as they toll the tidings that are to come. Hear the whispers as they pour forth from the mouths of all who seek wisdom in the name of the righteous One. Blend your energies into the matrix of Creation. Find the truths that are there for you to see. Feel the bastions of the many who come to watch, help, and enjoy the transmutations as they take form.

My beloveds, you have come to this time and place to be a part of the sequence of events that will turn the tide of humanity into new form. You have dwelled in this place, this place of servitude in a most dense situation. For that we are pleased. A new chapter is being written and you are the writers. You have called forth your brethren to turn the notch of creation up not only one level but many. Many of you have deemed necessary this time of creation in the form of extreme denseness. You have lived the lives bringing all of creation a new prospect that says all will prevail. You have prevailed and now you ask that you move on to new dimensions, to new ways of life. In your lives, the God aspect of yourselves, you have come to the conclusion that you are creation, you are the creators. There is no one but yourselves. You have the abilities to choose, change, transmute all energy.

You chose to go into the lower dimensions to fully understand life in form. When you choose such a rhythm you lose your knowledge of being a creator. This you have done and you will soon choose to awaken from your sleep. You will understand your connectedness to one another and to all of creation.

Love who you are and you will hear your own bells chime, not in the distance but within your own bodies. I Am that which you are. I Am the composite of all things. I Am love in action. Know that you will know this to be true. Know within your hearts you make up your own creations. You will know of this when you decide that love is the creation force. You will understand it is love that brings the wisdom to your being. It is the force that connects all.

Beloveds, the fall from grace is you forgetting who you are. Nothing can hold you down but yourselves. In gratitude, we of the star fleet on "human development" support you in all of your decisions. We will assist you only when called upon to bring about the changes you will soon desire. Know that indeed you are love in action.

February 29, 2004

Reunion

All time can be summed up as one large circle. What man creates today is taken from thoughts generated from other times, other lives, your life as well as lives of others. Life on this Earth has been cyclical. It has been contained, this force, this density. What man creates next may leap out of the circle. A new time is made. Get ready now and you will understand the words of this book. Namaste.

In the light of Most Radiant One, we come here to leave this message for you to gnaw on, to ponder. We are you in another time and space. Yet we leave you this message millions of years before you can comprehend the words. By leaving you this message in this time of Abraham, will you know that life is not linear. You will feel yourselves in this message. So sit back and feel the words you leave yourselves.

Acknowledge that you are a supreme being. Acknowledge that all and ever shall be is creation in your hands. Acknowledge that love in its highest vibration is what makes up the creative universe. Acknowledge that you are that love in action.

Masters, become aware of your abilities. Hear and see what you are. Come into balance and you shall see the makings of this universe. See the substrates of this miraculous land that you walk on. The embodiment of this great soul that you know as Terra acknowledges those masters who have come to be a part of her. Together you shall master the life form of man.

Oh, creator ones. Call upon the heavens so that they can take part in this development. They, too, are part of the total creation process. They were formed to assist the creator man in his web that he sets out in the heavens of heavens. All matter takes shape in the likeness of the trilogy of gamma. The waves of the mind that is the All appear to be sent out, but sent out of what? The All pervading force, the sparks of life that exists in everything. That is what the heavens are - sparks of life force. Arrange these sparks in a manner that will cause the life force to seize itself. Man has been given this ability to arrange these sparks. The mind goes into action and the sparks will align themselves as the thought gels into form. What happens to the form? It is only the thought. The thought can change, thus the form changes because it is the thought.

Masters of the universe, see yourselves as the grand creator. You are the tools of life. Open up your world and see yourselves in all aspects of your creation. Realize that creation cannot continue if you do not use your highest mind. Acknowledge that it is you, and that your body is only an expression of this mind. You will be able to look upon yourself as your only salvation. Connect with your higher spirit and flow forth the love that will permeate your body. Trust the sequence of events you have created and know that you will view all life as it truly is. Greet your many selves with love and thank them for their gifts. You will find you as the grand force in action. Love the possibilities and make your worlds in complete harmony with one another. You are the masters.

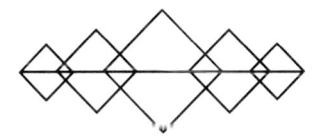

Q – What is meant (see paragraph four) by the sentence: "All matter takes shape in the likeness of the trilogy of gamma"?

A – Gamma is the third letter of the Greek alphabet and its numerical value is three. However, it means much more than that. It comes from the word "vessel" which means "to hold." Therefore in order for a vessel to manifest, there must be in place sparks of visceral energy that condenses upon reaching a frequency of 1,420 megahertz. This energy is stabilized using the electromagnetic force of the mind in conjunction with the magnetic mind of the living spectrum of Creator Force.

Simply said, gamma is the Creator mind working through the souls that inhabit this human body.

My mind does not totally comprehend this physics, therefore to gather more information on this is very difficult to download in my brain. Those of you who have a fuller understanding of gamma, gamma rays, frequencies, etc. may receive more information on this just by asking spirit.

May 30, 2004

Book of Nations

In this book shall it become known that all nations that comprise this Earth, even this galaxy, come from the forces of love. The vibrations of these beings radiate a form of brilliance. They encompass the worlds of form, yet they do not come from form. They are the brilliant white lights that move through the cosmos. They are sparks that know of themselves. They come together to experience new creations. They come as many yet they are as one in the making of new universes, new forms of life. They are the peacemakers of all creations. Blessings to them all. I shall speak from my own experiences, as I am a part of this process just as you are who read of these words.

The process of love is made manifest upon many planes of existence. The movement of the stars as they spin in their glory, each a part of the new life force that make up all creation. These forces are the sparks of divinity who move through the heavens making their lives as beings in the many forms of love.

The formation of great bodies of light are integers of the great sparks. They form their inherent energy base and take on a position of fine-tuning the seven aspects of the risen man into the Christ base of being. As man rises into a finer aspect of being, he will know that the future is a way to define new creation. He crosses into the state that defines all time into one level of consciousness yet the knowledge of being in the Christed state is but a step in the whole of Being. The thoughts of creation in the minds of man become the experience. Man thus defines his creation by means of his own thoughts and actions.

By the will of the great Creator shall the various life forms who make up the finer sparks of creation become the gods. In their processes shall they develop the necessary energy levels that will be the strength of new creations. They will form a new level that will adjust all other levels to move to a new position. These creator beings are the forces that have come from the stars. Their words, their actions, their deeds are their force in action. They combine with the thoughts of all others to become the new reality. This reality changes each moment. All moments change because each reality is and of itself. The new Earth shall be the stomping grounds of the ones who create from their base of knowledge. This base of knowledge is the universal laws of divine existence.

Creator ones have said that in their form shall the greatness of the cosmos become they who can love every part of their being, every part of all beings. They know of themselves to be the grand communicators that reach out into the star systems that light the earth's skies. They come as the inhabitors of fine grace within the stillness of their being. Within the reaches of the star systems that have a connection to the one of Earth has the call of light been extended. All lighted ones are to take their stations to receive the message that the call is out. Their consciousness shall focus on the earthen world. The earthen world shall be made up of the fine crystals which hold the divine sparks that shall be activated for the upliftment of all creation. Forces from the Andarean constellation come forth. Forces from the Sirian star come forth. Forces from the Octavius come forth. Forces from the realms of the divine Angelican come forth. Forces from the Arcturan system come forth. Forces from the realms of Andromeda come forth. Forces from all celestial nations that hold the frequency of creation in your light, come forth.

We shall come together to bring about a new way of being. It is a new time, a new life that brings a new knowledge of the forces of light.

With gratitude shall we come together, then spread out our forces. Let us combine our thoughts to bring about a great light that shall be known as the new Terra. The new Earth is to be reborn from the ashes of the worlds that are no more. This is a new place that shall be the ground for gods. With the input of great love in all of its aspects, this new world shall be the shining diamond of the cosmos. It has been spoken, therefore it is so.

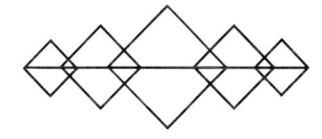

Q – What are the seven aspects of the risen man (see paragraph two)?
A – The seven aspects include the man's ability to cross the stations which his many selves inhabit. This means that he can cross into other lives – past, present, and future – of himself. He can cross into other dimensions, into other shapes of vessels (bodies), and into the void of existence where all life is.

The seven refers to the ability to move within the seven dimensions of physical existence. Once man knows that he can create all his existences, then man will know that life is love in action.

July 5, 2004

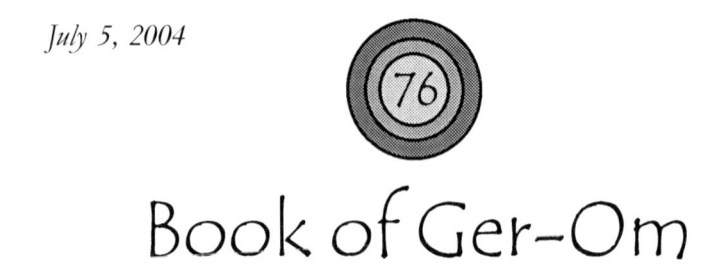

Book of Ger-Om

In the years before man was to become an intricate part of this world, the earth received an agreement that said that land was to become part of its body. It shall no longer hold the gases that caused it to burn inside. The soul of the cosmos divided itself and said that this gaseous body is to become an earthen body. It is to grow in its awareness and become a knowledgeable partner in the making of a new kingdom. In the agreement, it was to hold the making of elements that would withstand the forces of the powerful sun. It would hold its position in this galaxy, then turn and travel to a new place in the stars.

The first of the many changes started when the Great One said, "Let the time of a new day cast its shadow upon the worlds. Let the new become wisdom for many souls to grow and become a part of creatorship. Let the newness be a beacon for other manifestations to watch and receive new guidance. Let this be a world of salvation in that all life of this planet shall begin the process of making its own universe."

Because of this declaration, the forces of the other universes bond together their thoughts and actions to this new place, this new world.

As the changes progressed with the assistance of the gatekeepers, this new planet was born and the incoming soul, Gaia, took on a new plan, a new way of being. She knew of her role that she was to become a place where many civilizations would come together and hold her essence stable for others to bring their wares, their thoughts, their way of being. In this she rejoiced that she was to live so other lives could be fulfilled in the spirit. Matter was her manna. The life force entered every cell of this new planet. Her body vibrated with such magnitude that she burst forth a new energy. She attracted ones from thousands of planetary systems. They came to watch. They came to help. They came to be a part of the process.

What was to become of this new plan? Where will this new venture take creatorship? The many beings that came watched the new body spin as it pulled in debris from other systems that could not maintain their existence. Therefore, energetically, this earthen body is made up of body parts each bringing in their energetic influence.

Creator then said, "Let man be the dominion of the elements. Let man decipher their new lives. Let man return until it is finished."

Man is the machine that grows in its awareness. It is in the body that Creator can express creation in its finest degree. This body shall adapt itself to live with the other forms of life made by man and made by the forces of thought. With this process, life takes on a new twist. Life is the Creator and the created.

The stark new planet of choice is now in its final stages. It has come from its infancy into its adolescence. It has gained the knowledge of the thousands of star systems who have had a "hand" in its development. Gaia has come into her own power but refuses to dislodge humanity who have served her and in many cases have abused her. She rejoices at the fact that she has risen in her awareness of her own soul. She now will determine what is for her highest good, taking humanity with her. She will shake off those who are not in accordance to her plan. She will release those who have deceived her. She will maintain all who have come to assist her in her development as a star being. She has found her new frontier. She will move with grace into her new station. She will do so with the elegance of unrelenting love and protection of her peoples. She knows what she must do to realize her new commitment to the gentle forces of new creation. She begs for the reduction of needles in her skin. They are like a parasite to her. These needles are the machines that reduce her life flow, the oil wells that remove her precious substance, the blood of her life. She makes new blood to keep her body moving yet too much bloodletting can damage her.

In her movements to higher ways of being, she will receive increased vibrations to steady her for her next move into a new star system. Other planetary beings will assist her as she moves into place. She shall spin on her axis to hold her parts in place. Her moon will guide her. Along with her family, the neighboring planets that circle the sun will move with her. They, too, have their agendas and will become much greater in their own presence.

The glow that is given off by this planet and her friends is remarkable in that this movement is the result of the forces that have generated their life's energies into this new system. This new life has been an experiment of Creator of this part of this universe. Intricate forces from all of the contributing star systems have combined to form this new reality. A new level of understanding creator forces, creator energy has been accomplished. What now lies ahead is for this change, this growth-to-be is the undertaking of the higher forms of life to bring in their light where the lower forms of life exist. This creation shall move on with the knowing that a higher form of life is Creator's plan. May the sounds of the higher forms of life be heard and the changes begin.

Ger-Om –*The American Heritage Dictionary of the English Language,* Houghton, Mifflin Company, 1969: ger – to gather: to awaken

Om – sound of God

July 12, 2004

The Surrender to Manna

Manna, my friend, is the substance of All That Is. It is the life force, the God that exists in each and every one of you. It is your make-up. Surrender means to listen to your true self, to your God within. You came into this life time to bring about changes to hu-man and thus to all the worlds. You truly are an instrument of God and affect all of life. This book speaks of this and more. Thank you for listening. May your blessings flow.

The I (eye) is the god force that exists within every being that incarnates on the Earth plane. To acknowledge who and what you are, turn in and listen to your sound. The music you hear is your own individual print. Hear the music, the sounds. Listen care-fully and you will never have to ask another of your divinity. You will know why you have come (incarnated) upon this planet. You will walk in total knowingness of the intricacies of God, wisdom throughout your lives, in all dimensions, in all stations of your Life. You will understand that this place, this Earth is a speck of love in the wholeness of the universe. Yet, this Earth is an integral aspect of totality.

He who listens with divine intent shall relinquish the control he feels he must have over his life. He shall tune in and feel the flow of love throughout his being. Upon hearing the love that pours through the body, act upon the nudges of the universe. Act upon the love of prime Source. Act upon the wisdom received. He that does this will know of his total existence, his true being. Whatever one's contributions to the whole, know that it is you who is the dominate force of creation.

Masters of this Universe, feel the vibrations of this Earth. Hear her call and acknowledge her life force, her blood, her radiance. Man came to this planet to serve in the wholly position of entering into the new gate of supremacy. Each and every one of you is supreme in your being. You are an instrument of love to let the flow of minute particles pass through you to establish a new way of being. Act for your own self-interest. Each of you is your divine creator within the total matrix of the One, the Universe within the Universe within the Universe.

Feel your own significance. Feel your own strengths. Do not deny another's strengths but rejoice in knowing that each and every one has their own abilities, their own path, their own schedule. Respect all others and they shall respect you. Your power resides in your letting go of all restraints you may have put upon yourselves. Let your blessings flow. Blessings are there for all people, all religions, all walks of life.

We are you existing in another place and time. We look forward to the moment when we all come into focus of the total divine creation. We shall return to blend into the dimensional frequency that shall take us all to a new level of life. Listen and know that I Am God.

In divine love, we acknowledge the love force of Prime Creator.

June 27, 2004

Book of Peace

In an age where there is disharmony and injustice, the people will rally and say that life is not to be this way. They feel the imbalances and pray for change. Humanity's prayers are being answered. The time of social separation is coming to an end. Man shall know man for only what dwells in his heart. All hopes will become realities. The process of dualism has been part of the preparation of the new beginning. It has been shown that man can no longer tolerate the pettiness of others. He shall take his hand into his heart and bring all sides of himself together. An amazing celebration will be felt throughout the lands when man truly decides that unity is the answer to their prayers.

Dear ones, you are the writers of this book. You have been praying to me since my death many, many years ago. I came to teach balance. I came to teach that love is eternal and that each of you is part of that love. I came to teach that oneness is a result of the love. I came to say that man is just part of the total process. There are others who have a hand in this creation. Together you made a plan. Many call this the divine plan. This divine plan is your plan. Intricate lives are part of this human process. Every minute part of each of your lives has been to develop this land into something so great that all creations everywhere are watching. They know of the importance of this great project. They know the importance of each and very one of human kind.

Man, lay down all weapons. Lay down all hurts, all pain, all jealousies, all angers, all forms of separation. Do you not want peace? Peace is when all aspects of yourself are in order. Know that you have lived many lives and most every one of you have been the healers as well as the slayers. You have felt the injustices, the imbalances, and have played with them. That part of the project is over. It is time to move past all of your grievances and understand that life is ongoing. It is love in action.

The forests boast new life very day. Do you see yourself as part of a forest? You are of intrinsic value to every forest, every river, every mineral on this planet. You are part of the planet herself. She weeps when you do not understand that she is a living entity. She lives for you, her life partners. She depends upon you for her support. She breathes through her nostrils. They are her land, her body. She groans for the total love and acceptance as a beautiful being. She has such deep love for you that she is delaying her progress into the upper levels of life until you, man, is ready.

Holy, holy are we that we all are in this project together. We came here for a purpose and that purpose is being fulfilled. Break all promises that do not serve your purpose anymore. Come to the forefront of your life. Pray for unity and you shall see that unity. Open your hearts and see what is to be. Your lives are endless. You are eternal so get used to it. Know that you have been kept in bondage in my name. Cut the strings. I, too, shall feel freer. I am here for you, humankind. I am here for us. Let us fly and feel the freedom that we all will possess. The countdown has started. Are you going to join me?

With love and respect, I AM Sananda, operator of the fifth ray of unity. Let us begin now.

August 3, 2003

Book of the New Tomorrow

This book begins at a time of transfiguration. The "time" period is now, from August 18, 2003, until the end of time, the month of darkness – December 28, 2011 - to the return of the light. Light at that moment will look different in that the golden spectrum will have a rosy glow. The sky will take on a more green/blue appearance. The oceans will look more aqua. It is the new beginning in a new world full of a new way of being.

The moment of transfiguration of the Earth plane will be in the Age of Aquarius. At that time there will be junctures of the planets of the solar system that will turn planets on their sides, move them out of their position, and rearrange this part of our galaxy. Streams of light matter will be seen in the skies that herald the return of the ancient One of Old who will be the transmitter of the new plan.

The New Tomorrow is the New Age. It is an age where all is in accordance to divine laws in the name of the One. It is also a place. Ones who know of their lineage, the starseeds, shall be the first to awaken into the new consciousness. They shall be the prototypes of the new Earth. All of humankind shall traverse the dimensions into the knowing of the divine seed. They shall know of the Father Universe and of the Mother Universe. They shall know of the beginnings and the end. They shall know of existence much larger than they think they know themselves. They shall be the forerunners of many new civilizations.

They shall accept the knowledge of the beleaguered. They know of the truths that all are in this together and nothing shall deter them from their paths. They shall know of the secrets that much knowledge was kept from them yet they shall feel that impending need to know that they are part of something much larger than what they see, hear, touch, and smell.

The Ones of Old shall return to remember the patterns. Within the patterns are the new worlds leading to new lives. Anticipation that all will be made new in the name of the mother/father, a universal concept of all that Is. They will return into the sacred patterns to bring in the new patterning. When the hour arrives, multitudes will lift up their hearts, their minds in the area of creatorship, knowing that is what they have done all along.

The masses shall turn their faces toward the heavens for the Ancient Ones shall return in their fiery grandeur. They shall come unto the masses with their light of gold. They will come in the midst of despair to bring about the change of light bursting forth from our dear Mother Earth, our Gaia of old as she births the new Terrain.

Such glorious tales shall these be when mankind realizes their position in the divine creed. The ship of Malduk shall return into these parts to further awaken mankind. Their fiery ways will frighten some but with the love of creator in the hearts of those who have awakened will lessen the ache in the frightened bellies. The masks will be removed. May the many forces make themselves known.

Wise ones, leave the imprints of this knowledge in the crystal makeup of their earthen body. Code into them that the return of the ancients will be showing themselves upon the turn of this grand solar system of divine light. Release and rise into the mists that have veiled man from his greater knowledge. This book is but a reminder that shall be released from its hiding when man must take a step in their evolution. May all who hear of these writings feel the golden arrows pierce their hearts. They shall know that truly they are their Creators.

Beauty of the light shall illuminate all corners of darkness. No rock shall be left unturned. The oracles shall take their place. Speak of the gladness that is befalling the Earth. Walk in assurance that the new day is with them. Beings from the many heavens shall take their place in the opening of all records. Glory shall abound in all things, all things. Those who hear these words shall know that indeed, the New Day is here.

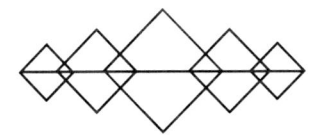

Q – Who and what is the ship of Malduk?

A – The ship of Malduk is the ship that belongs to, or is a part of, the system you call Sirius. The beings who control this ship have been part of the Earth process through the many incarnations of the Earth's peoples. These beings are the fornicators of this vast system of souls who have volunteered to be a part of the hu-man experiment. By fornicators, we mean that they have assisted this process of evolution to benefit all of Creator's creations. This process we call interpenetration of all souls is the process of soul evolution in its highest degree. The creation processes on this great planet of Gaia is an incredible experiment of souls coming into a system where they know not who and what they are capable of. This has been an extraordinary experiment that has surprised even the most skeptical of evolved beings.

As you human beings learn more about your heritage and understand your significance, you will soon attain the knowledge and wisdom that you all have within yourselves. That is the way it is written and that is as it should be. You are the wayshowers of future generations on this earth and other planetary bodies.

July 19, 2004

The Greatest Story Ever Told

This indeed is the greatest story ever told. No, it is not about my life as Jeshua ben Joseph (Jesus) but about you, all of you who have incarnated at this juncture to bring about the true peace and understanding of your divinity. You shall move mountains, you shall travel not only on this planet, but to many other planets. You shall migrate to places unseen and unheard of. This and much more awaits you. Are you ready?

Greetings in the light of the Most Radiant One. You who read of these words and feel the thoughts as they pour through you, know that you were chosen to be one of those beings who came to this planet to be of assistance. Know in your hearts and minds that this trip to this place and time has been on your schedule for eons. Know that you have been led here by your thoughts integrating with other thoughts of this grand plan of ascension.

Did you know that time does not really exist? It is just a construct to bring you to this point of realization that all that you see, hear, taste, smell, and feel are a microcosm of what you really are. Your senses far exceed the five physical senses. You will understand when your other twelve senses come into your awareness. Yes, twelve is the magic number coupled with the five that will bring you to the realization that this universe is just a stop on the way to the manifestation of the many galaxies and other universes that too are constructs of the heart and mind. I can hear you saying, "Whoa, what are you talking about? Many universes we are making? Explain this. That is powerful stuff!"

Powerful is each and every one of you. Never doubt who and what you are. Resign to the fact that it is you who are the decision-makers, the planners, and the designers. Clarity of your mind and body are the opportunities for you to grasp the meaning of such a statement. Clear out the debris that has accumulated through your lives on this planet as well as your lives on many of the other planets in this galaxy and thousands of others.

Each of you is a thread that is a connection to everything that exists now and forever more. You are an integral part of the whole, with every one no less and no more than your fellow souls. Understand the message that you are no less and no more than anyone, anywhere, any time. You each have your own agenda, and that agenda may change as one aspect of your creation is finished to begin the next aspect.

There are twelve layers of existence. Each layer has within it the ability to co-create life forms. These creative forces form the center of all creation. Each thread that you occupy is attached to this center so every thought and action are recorded and felt by all souls that are part of this center. Once you have realized your true abilities and have mastered love in divine creation, then you move onto the next layer of existence. Again you are a golden thread that is attached to the center of all creation (in that layer). Creation is endless as there really is no time. Space can be defined as that which one perceives as an area within his sphere. Therefore space and time are guides for your creations.

Freedom is yours to engage in the experience of your creations as well as other souls within your layer. Every thought and action affects all within each layer. It is up to each and every soul in your layer to take into himself or herself the thought or just let it go by. If a thought is not for the highest good of all the souls, then that thought will dissipate. It will be absorbed and transmuted by the higher thoughts of other souls. The term "higher" means that the energy created by a thought is a more refined energy which vibrates at a faster rate. Everything is energy in motion.

Once the five senses of taste, smell, touch, hear, and see are mastered, then the sixth sense of perception and intuition will become heightened. This sixth sense enables one to more easily connect to other souls. The remaining eleven senses contribute to the connection to the center of the creation layer. The first five senses will become heightened in their intensity. The feeling of being in one place will change and you will be able to perceive your other lives simultaneously. Wherever you put your attention, then that life or time will be highlighted and your thoughts will be centered on that time or place. Initial confusion will take place but this sixth sense will also be mastered and your creative abilities seen as what they truly are.

Your dreams and your goals in each life will be attained unless those goals are not in alignment with the central source in your creation layer. To understand alignment is divine love in the upliftment of all souls. Therefore know that Source will only permit the higher vibrational thought patterns to exist. Any "lower" thoughts or vibrations will be transmuted. It is the free choice of all souls to create from their hearts and minds, but choosing the lower thought forms will keep one from knowing and understanding the movement of creation.

They will remain in a pattern until they are ready to transcend into a higher vibrational mode of being.

You who have come to this planet Earth, came to assist in transcending the lower vibrations so that each and every being can move into the next vibration in understanding and experiencing creation. Each soul in this layer of Creation can then move on in the making of new creations of love made manifest. Your abilities are endless and, with the increased vibrations of the once lower thought forms, your senses will be enhanced and the true knowledge of your being be understood.

We are the Light Bearers. We work with all beings who have come to this planet of free choice to assist in the harmony of the worlds.

Index

Abraham 35, 57-59, 69, 70, 95, 100, 102, 125, 147, 154, 155, 201, 203, 220
adam 48, 50, 71, 131, 170 - 171, 179, 216
adamic seed 170
adrenal glands 103, 105, 128
Airophim 70
Akashic Records 11, 74
Akhtum 35
Albaktan 103, 105 - 106
aliens 20
Anami 51 - 52
Andromeda 28, 32 - 33, 151, 225
anphybium 60
Antares 25, 27, 33
Antibus 82 - 83
Anunnaki 138, 154
Arcturus 25, 27, 32 - 33, 117, 151
Aristotle 156, 190
Artemis 158 - 159
Ashtar Command 196
Atlantis 36, 57, 82
atoms 116, 121 - 122, 124, 131, 160
atum 46
Babylon 69, 72
Bekeleh 146, 203, 206
Bethlehem 68, 200
bio-genesis 136
blood 39, 127, 228, 230
brain 15, 115, 127 - 128, 222
Brotherhood of Creative Forces 29 - 30
Bruins 12, 13
catalyst 14, 83, 134
cells 5, 7, 30, 60, 108, 116, 123 - 124, 133, 208
Cleaus 170 - 171

Council of Five 119
Council of Nun 92
crystal(s), crystalline structures 83, 111, 112, 115-117, 127, 130-132, 151, 163, 171, 201, 234
Cydonia 68, 71
diode(s) 14, 16
DNA 60, 211
dolphins 27
electromagnetic 10, 104, 121 - 122, 127, 158, 164, 199, 211, 213, 222
electrons 4, 113, 116, 121, 131
Elohim 13, 59, 69, 71, 137, 201
endorphins 103
Ereocles 130
Essenes 12, 16 - 17, 19, 22
Eurocles 50, 212, 214
Eve 154, 216
Evil 63, 66, 94, 187-189
flower of life 205
forgiveness 187
fusion 83, 108, 134, 218
Gaia 17, 61, 66 - 67, 74, 102, 115 - 116, 126, 127, 140, 149, 154, 165, 170 - 171, 199, 217, 226 - 227, 234 - 235
Galactic Council of Seven 2, 4
Galeceans 68
Garden of Eden 114
Geldeiah 96, 98 - 99
gematrian body of light 133-135
genetic(s), geneticists 31, 33, 68, 115, 125, 207
geometry 11, 70, 124
Gods of Abroc 124 - 125
Gods of Turan 147, 149, 203, 206
grids 69, 124, 195
Hall of Records 11, 119

heaven(s) 6 - 7, 10, 13, 19, 23 - 24, 41, 56, 58, 70, 76, 90-92, 96, 101, 108, 113 -114, 146 - 147, 156, 164, 167-170, 172, 178, 189, 196, 199, 204, 207, 210, 213, 221, 223, 234 - 235
heman 108 - 109
Holy Alcyone 133-135
Holy Grail 51 - 52, 118, 146, 198, 215
Holy Sepulcher 202, 204
hypothalamus 15, 128
in-breath 118 - 119, 214
infinity 66, 131
ions 14, 118, 121, 160-162
Isis 1
Jehovah 44, 142
Jerusalem 58, 136 - 137, 198, 203, 206
Jesus 66, 130, 166, 237
Jupiter 137, 151, 171
Knights of Templar 84
kundalini 60
Lemuria 103, 105
Library of Delphin 156, 196
Light Ship Athena 193, 196
living liquid light 31 - 32
Lleken 126, 146 - 147, 149
magnetics 66, 120, 161, 195
Mais 199, 201
Malduk 234 - 235
manna 25 - 26, 169, 171, 227, 229
Mars 68, 71 - 72, 171
medulla oblongata 115 - 116
Melchizedek 10, 216
Mercury 151
merkaba 24
Milky Way Galaxy 62
mineral kingdom 26, 112
molecules 111, 118

Monrovian Beings 88, 90
moon 48 - 49, 115 - 116, 120, 158, 162, 228
nautilus 209-211
Nefilim (Nephilim) 136-138
nether 8
neutrons 4, 113, 131-133
nimion 13
nuclear fusion 83, 218
Orion 25, 27, 33, 70, 90, 100, 133, 213 - 214
Osiris 10, 101
out-breath 118 - 119, 162, 214
People of Jezbel 25
photon(s) 108, 111, 120 - 121
photosynthesis 116
physics 79, 143, 156, 222
pineal copular resonance 14, 16
pineal gland 16, 103, 105
pituitary gland 128
plasma 121
Pleiades 25, 27, 32 - 33, 90, 151, 214
protons 4, 31, 113, 131 - 132
protosynthesis 104, 106
Ra 153
rapture 2
reproduction 26, 65, 80, 103, 105
sacred geometry 11, 124
Sagittarius 108
salvation 9, 11, 55, 184, 221, 226
Sananda 1, 8, 47, 57, 59 - 60, 68, 71, 103, 107, 111, 148, 160, 163, 167, 184, 232
Saturn 151, 171
seventh heaven 23, 24
seventh sun 28, 136, 138
Sirius 26 - 27, 32 - 33, 60, 90, 214, 235
Sodulites 151

Solaris 154
Soltecs 12, 13
Song of the messiah 165
star matrix 22, 24
Star Ship Acillia 28
Sumer xv
sun 1, 3, 9, 23, 25, 27-30, 32, 34,
    48 - 49, 57, 69, 80 - 81, 83, 104,
    120, 124, 130 - 131, 136, 138,
    151, 158, 161 - 162, 164, 170,
    175 - 176, 178, 212, 213, 226,
    228
Terra 2, 32, 35, 190 - 191, 199, 216
    - 217, 220, 225
The Crusades 86
The Federation of Light 67
The Galactic Federation 67
The Great Central Sun 1, 3, 9, 28,
    31, 104, 130, 131, 164
transfiguration 28, 83, 233
Twelve Tribes of Israel xv
Urion 177, 210
Venus 151
vessel 222
vineral energy 116 - 117
wayshowers 13, 53, 73, 236
whales 27
YHWH 76
zep tepi 133
Zeus 159

Notes